NATIVE AMERICANS

DISCOVER THE HISTORY & CULTURES OF THE FIRST AMERICANS

WITH 15 PROJECTS

Kim Kavin

Illustrated by Beth Hetland

~ Latest titles in the *Build It Yourself* Series ~

Check out more titles at www.nomadpress.net

Nomad Press
A division of Nomad Communications
10 9 8 7 6 5 4 3 2 1

This book was manufactured by Sheridan Books, Ann Arbor, MI USA.
June 2013, Job # 347613
ISBN: 978-1-61930-175-7

Illustrations by Beth Hetland
Educational Consultant, Marla Conn

Questions regarding the ordering of this book should be addressed to
Independent Publishers Group
814 N. Franklin St.
Chicago, IL 60610
www.ipgbook.com

Nomad Press
2456 Christian St.
White River Junction, VT 05001
www.nomadpress.net

Contents

Timeline

20,000 BCE–8000 BCE
It is believed that the first Americans arrive in the Americas within this 12,000-year period and live as hunter-gatherers.

13,000 BCE–11,000 BCE
Scientists date artifacts found in Oregon, Chile, and New Mexico to this period.

5000 BCE–3500 BCE
People in Mesoamerica, in the area that is now called Mexico, are farming maize, squash, beans, and potatoes, and have learned to make pottery.

3000 BCE People begin living north of the Arctic Circle.

1500 BCE Paintings at Pictograph Cave in Montana are dated to this period.

1200 BCE The Anasazi are living in pit houses in the Southwest.

1000 BCE Hufe earthen mounds are built by the Adena in Ohio, Pennsylvania, and New York, and the Olmecs are building temple pyramids.

400 BCE–1500 CE The Hohokam culture rises to prominence in the Southwest.

300 BCE–1300 CE The Mogollon culture rises to prominence in the Rocky Mountains.

100 CE It is believed that Teotihuacán, an Aztec city, houses 200,000 people.

200 CE Tikal, a Maya city, spans 23 miles.

1000 Tikal and Teotihuacán have fallen by this time for unknown reasons.

1300–1400 As many as 500,000 Iroquois and Algonquians live in the Northeast Woodlands and Great Lakes regions. It is believed that this was the height of these civilizations.

1400–1500 European explorers arrive in North America.

1492 European explorer Christopher Columbus makes landfall in the Americas and describes finding "Indians."

1513 European explorer Juan Ponce de León makes landfall in modern-day Florida.

1620 The Mayflower lands at Plymouth Rock.

1621 The pilgrims and Native Americans share a feast that later becomes the basis for Thanksgiving.

1650 About 50,000 Cherokee live in the Southeast, in as many as 200 villages.

1680 Popé leads the Pueblo Revolt.

1741 Vitus Bering dies trying to find a land bridge between Siberia and North America. His ship's crew bring back beaver pelts, beginning a fashion fad that inspires many Europeans to set sail for America's Pacific Northwest.

JULY 4, 1776 The Declaration of Independence is signed, establishing the independence of the original 13 colonies.

1804–1806 Lewis and Clark make their famous expedition.

1828 The *Cherokee Phoenix*, the first Native American newspaper, is published.

1829 U.S. President Andrew Jackson declares that there is an "Indian Problem."

1830 Andrew Jackson signs the Indian Removal Act.

1838 Roughly 15,000 Cherokees in Georgia, North Carolina, and Tennessee are forced to relocate. They have to leave their homes and walk the "Trail of Tears" to Oklahoma.

Timeline

1843–1852 Governor Isaac Stevenson of the Washington Territory negotiates 52 treaties that transfer 157 million acres of land from Native Americans to the United States.

1858–1886 Geronimo, an Apache warrior, leads raids against Mexican and U.S. settlements.

1864 Groups of Navajo are forced to walk over 400 miles and relocate near Fort Sumner in New Mexico.

1876 Sitting Bull and Crazy Horse lead a battle against U.S. Lt. Col. George Armstrong Custer: the Battle of Little Bighorn, a.k.a. "Custer's Last Stand."

1900 By the start of the century less than a thousand buffalo remain alive in North America. One hundred years earlier there had been an estimated 60 million.

1905 U.S. President Theodore Roosevelt invites Geronimo to participate in a Washington, DC, parade.

1929 James Ridgley Whiteman finds spear points and new evidence of a flourishing Native American culture that existed thousands of years before the European settlers arrived in the "New World."

1939–1945 During World War II, Navajo Wind Talkers enable the U.S. military to communicate in codes that baffle German and Japanese code breakers.

1964 The Civil Rights Act restores tribal law on reservations.

1970 President Richard Nixon, in a speech to Congress titled "Special Message on Indian Affairs," calls for a new era of self-determination for native peoples.

1978 The American Indian Religious Freedom Act becomes U.S. law, making native religious practices legal again.

1980 The U.S. Supreme Court rules that the Sioux Indians are entitled to $17.5 million, plus 5 percent interest per year since 1877, totaling about $106 million, for the taking of the Black Hills against the promises of the Treaty of Fort Laramie.

1988 The Indian Gaming Regulatory Act allows reservations to build casinos and offer gaming to the general public.

1996 President Bill Clinton declares that every November shall be National American Indian Heritage Month.

2002 With construction under way on the National Museum of the American Indian in Washington, DC, 500 Native Americans dance during a nearby two-day powwow attended by 25,000 spectators.

2004 The National Museum of the American Indian opens in Washington, DC.

DID YOU KNOW?!
Whether inventing ways to preserve fish without refrigeration, creating houses out of snow, or training horses to become effective partners in battle, Native Americans continually shaped new ideas that remain a strong influence on people all over the world today.

Native People

It was well over 10,000 years ago that Native Americans first arrived in North America. No one knows exactly when they came, but it was long before European explorers arrived. If you flip through an old United States history book, you'll find that the first people of the **Americas** were often portrayed as **savages**. Today, of course, we know this was not at all true.

In fact, Native Americans have always been hardworking, clever people who lived in harmony with the natural world around them. The way they lived, and the tools they created and used along the way, is a tribute to the human spirit.

All the different **tribes** had to **adapt** their homes, **cultures**, and methods of survival to their **environment**. They were so successful that huge **civilizations** emerged.

WORDS TO KNOW

Americas: the lands of North and South America.

savage: fierce, uncontrolled, and ferocious.

tribe: a large group of people with common **ancestors** and **customs**.

ancestors: people from your family or culture that lived before you.

customs: traditions or ways of doing things, including dress, food, and holidays.

adapt: to make changes to survive in new or different conditions.

culture: the beliefs and way of life of a group of people.

environment: a natural area with plants and animals.

civilization: a community of people that is advanced in art, science, and politics.

theory: an unproven idea used to explain something.

◈ **Where did the first Americans come from? How did they travel to the Americas? No one knows for sure but we'll take a look at the _theories_.**

In this book, we'll explore the history of the first people who made their homes on the land we know today as the United States. We'll trace their progress from small groups of people making tools out of stone and driftwood into large civilizations with complex calendars, intricate art, deep spiritual beliefs, and written and spoken languages.

Of the many hundreds of Native American tribes, we will focus on a few groups. Their lifestyles, shelters, and tools show survival methods and cultures in different parts of the Americas.

Among them are the Inuit, who learned how to survive near the Arctic Circle. The Cherokee dominated much of the Southeast and developed a written language that spread across the continent. The Tlingit discovered and reaped the benefits of **trade** in goods all across the Pacific Northwest.

The story of these and other Native American cultures is not just a story of survival, but of **ingenuity** and adaptation in the face of great challenges.

WORDS TO KNOW

trade: to exchange goods for other goods or money.

ingenuity: the ability to solve difficult problems creatively.

ARCTIC

INUIT

PACIFIC NORTHWEST

NUU-CHAH-NULTH, MAKAH, TLINGIT

NORTHEAST WOODLANDS

GREAT PLAINS

CHEYENNE, LAKOTA SIOUX, COMANCHE

ALGONQUIAN, IROQUOIS

HOPI, APACHE, NAVAJO

SOUTHWEST

GREAT LAKES

SOUTHEAST

MESOAMERICA

MAYA, AZTEC

CHEROKEE, CATAWBA, CREEK, SEMINOLE

CHAPTER 1

The First Americans

How did your family come to live where you live? Were you born there, or did you and your family move by plane, by car, or by train? Why does your family live in one state instead of another? Did your grandparents or great-grandparents come from another country and travel across the ocean to get here?

Scientists are trying to understand how the earliest people got to North America at all. Experts have traced human history back to long before your great-great grandparents lived, to the time when the very first people made their way across vast stretches of ocean to the Americas. It wasn't 20 years ago. It wasn't 200, or even 2,000 years ago. The best guess is that it was 10,000 or maybe even 20,000 years ago.

◆ **These were the earliest Native Americans, the very first people to live on the North American continent.**

There was no United States of America back then. There were no countries, just the landmasses that we now call North and South America. This land is separated by the Atlantic and Pacific Oceans from Europe and Asia, where the first human beings appear to have lived. Somehow, and for some reason, groups of these people **migrated** across the oceans. They had no maps or cars, and there were no roads or signs to guide them.

The first people to arrive had only themselves and the **natural resources** around them. With no seeds to plant, they had to hunt the animals roaming the **wilderness** and catch the fish swimming in the rivers. These people had to adapt. They learned when it would be hot and when it would be cold, and figured out how to get food and shelter for their families in each season.

MIGRATION ROUTES

If you look at a map of the world, you'll see a narrow body of water that we called the Bering Strait separating Alaska and Russia. North of the Bering Strait is the Arctic Ocean. It's the smallest ocean in the world, but still nearly one and a half times the size of the United States. South of the Bering Strait is the Pacific Ocean, which is the biggest ocean in the world. It separates the west coast of the United States from Japan, China, and all of Asia. Modern ships can easily cross the Pacific Ocean, but the journey takes days.

How would the earliest Native Americans have migrated across either the Arctic Ocean or the Pacific Ocean? They would have risked freezing to death in the Arctic, and the Pacific is enormous. It's hard to believe that over 10,000 years ago people could have constructed boats that were sturdy enough to make such a difficult journey.

So how did they get here?
And why did they come in the first place?

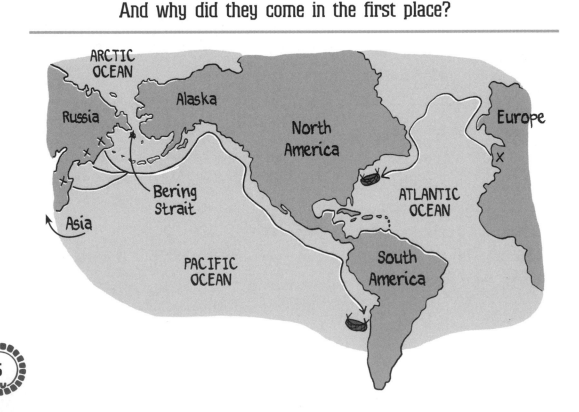

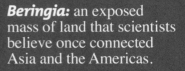

According to one theory, there was once a visible mass of land between Asia and the Americas. We call this land **Beringia**. The theory is that Beringia appeared near the end of an **Ice Age**. Because seawater was frozen in great sheets of ice, land that had been underwater was exposed.

ARCTIC OCEAN

Russia

Beringia

Alaska

PACIFIC OCEAN

Scientists think Beringia was about 1,240 miles long, a little bit longer than California's coastline (almost 2,000 kilometers), and that it was covered in grasses and other plants. Animals eat grass and plants. In those days, wherever animals went, so did people, because animals were a major source of food.

DID YOU KNOW?

Some **evidence** suggests there may have been migrations of people by boat from Asia to South America, and from Europe to the East Coast of North America. These seagoing migrants could have island-hopped by boat across the Pacific Rim, or iceberg-hopped across the Atlantic.

So when animals began to cross Beringia from Asia to North America, people followed. And they stayed. Maybe they liked the new countryside they found. Or maybe the ice sheets began to melt and the water level rose above the land bridge. Or perhaps the hunters followed the animals so far south that they never went back.

FINDING FOOD

If you find some of today's wild animals intimidating, imagine hunting the **megafauna** living in the Americas when the first people arrived. Giant armadillos, mastodons, reindeer, saber-toothed tigers, and long-horned bison were much bigger than any of their relatives living today. Beavers are thought to have been the size of modern-day grizzly bears. Woolly mammoths weighed 3 tons and stood 14 feet tall (over 4 meters). That's higher than the ceiling in most of today's homes.

WORDS TO KNOW

megafauna: an animal weighing more than 100 pounds (45 kilograms).

Mammoth or Mastodon?

• •

Do you know the difference between a mammoth and a mastodon? Both were huge animals with tusks that are related to today's elephants. These animals roamed the earth from about 1.8 million years ago until about 10,000 years ago. Evidence of mastodons has been found on every continent except Antarctica and Australia. Mammoths lived in cold northern climates and came to North America across the Bering Land Bridge.

Both of these animals were enormous, but mammoths were bigger. The largest mastodons reached a mere 10 feet tall (3 meters). The mastodon's tusks were straighter and much shorter than the mammoth's. A mammoth's curved tusks could reach up to 13 feet long (4 meters), compared to a mastodon's 8-foot tusks (2½ meters).

There is evidence that early Native Americans hunted these massive animals using tools made of bone and stone. That's an impressive feat since these tips had to go through hair, skin, and muscle up to a foot thick (30 centimeters).

Just one of these massive animals fed many people for months. But killing the large beasts wasn't easy without guns or bows and arrows. Native Americans became better hunters when they figured out how to make sharp, pointed spears that they could throw. In addition to hunting, it's likely that people fished, collected shellfish, and gathered wild fruit and vegetables.

They made tools with whatever they could find. It's likely they used short sticks with sharp ends to dig up roots and to pry open clams and other shellfish. Long sticks could be used to knock down fruit from high in the trees. There is evidence that containers made from leaves, tree bark, and animal skins were used to carry food.

DID YOU KNOW?

There was another furry animal hunted by early humans called the woolly rhino. It roamed the plains of Europe and northern Asia until about 8000 BCE.

CLOVIS CULTURE

Many **archaeologists** have spent their lives studying the **relics** left behind by the earliest Native Americans. These relics are sometimes buried under thousands of years' worth of **debris**, but they are the only clues we have as to how the earliest Native Americans got here and how they lived.

WORDS TO KNOW

archaeologist: a scientist who studies ancient people and their cultures through the objects they left behind.

relic: an item used by people in an earlier time.

debris: the remains of anything broken down or destroyed.

9

In the 1930s, deep underground in a place called Clovis, New Mexico, archaeologists found the remains of animals that had been **extinct** for thousands of years. All around the remains, they found beautifully carved spear points made from rocks that people had shaped and sharpened. The pointed rocks were sometimes tied to the ends of long sticks and used for hunting.

◈ These became known as Clovis points, and there are more than 25 known Clovis caches, or groups of these carved spear points, in North America.

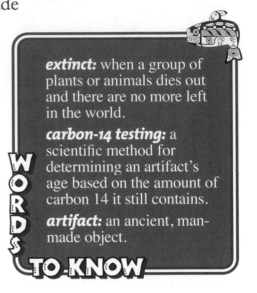

WORDS TO KNOW

extinct: when a group of plants or animals dies out and there are no more left in the world.

carbon-14 testing: a scientific method for determining an artifact's age based on the amount of carbon 14 it still contains.

artifact: an ancient, man-made object.

Carbon-14 testing dated the **artifacts** left behind by the Clovis culture to over 13,000 years ago. This led experts to believe that the Clovis people were the very first people in the Americas. In 1977, however, older remains were found in South America in Monte Verde, Chile. Relics such as tent poles, burned wood, animal hides, and even mastodon meat dated back before the Clovis culture. Other sites predating Clovis have since been discovered in North America. Scientists have dated human remains found in the Paisley Caves in Oregon to over 14,000 years ago.

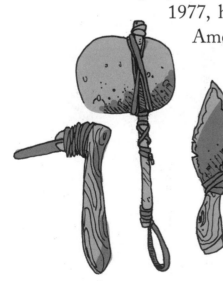

Carbon-14 Testing

Archaeologists study ancient life and cultures by *excavating* and studying relics and artifacts that ancient people have left behind. But when archaeologists find something old, such as a wooden spoon or a spear point, how do they know exactly how old it is?

They use a scientific process called carbon-14 testing. All living things, including trees and other plants and animals, absorb a *radioactive element* called carbon-14, or C-14 for short. C-14 doesn't hurt the plants or animals. In fact, a little bit of C-14 seeps in every day.

When the living thing dies, the absorbed C-14 starts to break down. It's like tiny, *microscopic* crumbs falling off a cookie until the cookie is eventually gone. It may take thousands of years for that cookie to disappear completely, but it's crumbling a tiny bit more every day.

Scientists can measure C-14 so precisely that they can tell how old something is based on the rate of C-14 breakdown. A wooden spoon with a moderate amount of C-14 left may be hundreds of years old, while a wooden spoon still containing only microscopic amounts of C-14 may be thousands of years old.

WORDS TO KNOW

excavate: to dig up.

radioactive element: a chemical substance made of one type of atom that changes because its positively charged particles escape from its center over time.

microscopic: something so small it can only be seen with a microscope.

TOOLS

The earliest Native Americans made rocks and bones into tools by banging and sharpening them with other rocks. Some of the tools were uniface, meaning only one side of the rock had been sharpened. Other tools were biface, with both sides of the rock sharpened. Spear points and knives were biface, since banging away at both sides of a rock resulted in a sharper tip. Uniface tools were better for things like scraping animal meat off of bones and for making other tools.

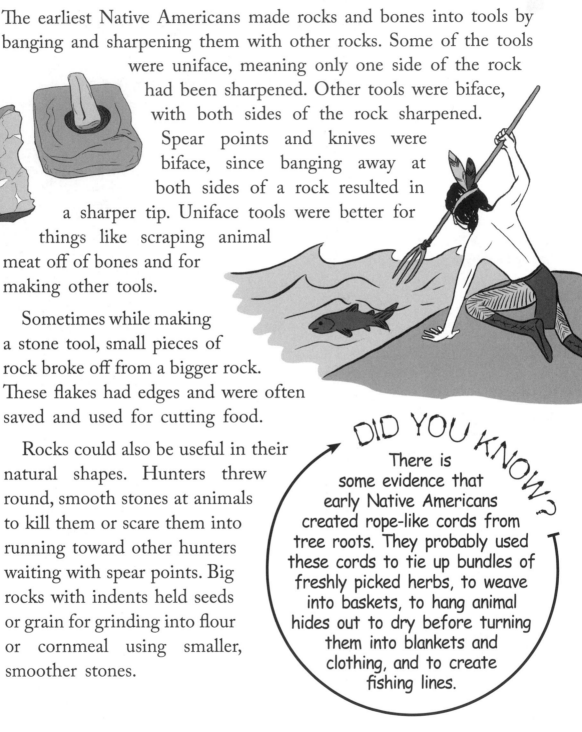

Sometimes while making a stone tool, small pieces of rock broke off from a bigger rock. These flakes had edges and were often saved and used for cutting food.

Rocks could also be useful in their natural shapes. Hunters threw round, smooth stones at animals to kill them or scare them into running toward other hunters waiting with spear points. Big rocks with indents held seeds or grain for grinding into flour or cornmeal using smaller, smoother stones.

DID YOU KNOW?

There is some evidence that early Native Americans created rope-like cords from tree roots. They probably used these cords to tie up bundles of freshly picked herbs, to weave into baskets, to hang animal hides out to dry before turning them into blankets and clothing, and to create fishing lines.

The Slug Blade

• •

Not long after the earliest Native Americans learned how to make sharp blades out of rock, they began to create blades of different shapes and sizes for different tasks.

What's amazing is that the big blades were all very similar to one another, as were all the small blades and thin blades. How did they make the blades turn out the same every time? They had a simple but clever idea. They chipped away at both sides of a large rock until it was twice the width they wanted their blades to be. Then they split the rock in half by banging the top of it with another rock. The result of this impact would be two, nearly identical blade tools. French archaeologists named this type of tool *limace*, which means "slug." With the flat side down, that's what the blade looks like—a slug.

ROCK ART

Some experts believe that the first Native American artwork came from excitement around an upcoming animal hunt, just like you might get psyched up before a big soccer game today. **Petroglyphs** and **pictographs** have been found on boulders and in caves all over North America. Some of the images are simple geometric shapes like circles, dots, and sunbursts. Others show plants, Native American headdresses, and human and animal figures.

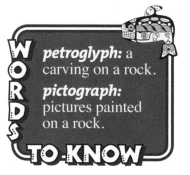

WORDS TO KNOW

petroglyph: a carving on a rock.

pictograph: pictures painted on a rock.

Paintings of animals and warriors over 3,500 years old have been found in Pictograph Cave in Montana. Petroglyphs of corn stalks were found in cliffs in Colorado. The Chumash people created elaborate rock art in southern California depicting images of humans, animals, and the sun and stars, while a group of adults and children that appear to be dancing, drumming, and singing was discovered on the Narrows rock panel in Arkansas.

WORDS TO KNOW

pigment: a substance found in nature that can be used to give color to paint.

fiber: a short thread.

forage: to search for food.

society: an organized community of people.

Petroglyphs were made by carving a rock's surface with another stone. Pictographs were made with natural **pigments** made from ground-up minerals. Hematite was used to make red, limonite for yellow, kaolin clays for white, and charcoal for black. Mixing the powders with animal fat, egg whites, fish or plant oil, or blood made paint. People used their fingers or brushes made from twigs or plant **fibers**.

NATIVE AMERICAN CULTURE

Carrying water from the stream, setting up and breaking down campsites, hunting, **foraging** for plants to eat, and making clothing were all necessary daily activities. This is how life was—all work and no play. But that would change as new generations of Native Americans developed more complex **societies** and cultures.

UNDERSTANDING
THE ICE AGE

Scientists believe that during the Ice Age, much of the world's seawater was frozen into great sheets of ice. This made the oceans shallower, since there was less melted water to fill them up. You can duplicate this yourself using ice cream.

1 Place a scoop of ice cream into your bowl. Notice that when the ice cream is frozen in a ball, you can still see the bowl beneath it. During the Ice Age, the land on the ocean floors was exposed in the same way, with all the water frozen on top.

2 Now, let your ice cream melt. Watch how the melted ice cream covers the bottom of your bowl, just like the earth's giant blocks of ice melted to cover the ocean floor. If you had a big enough scoop of ice cream, it would melt enough to fill up the entire bowl, just as the world's seawater has filled up the oceans today.

SUPPLIES

- ice cream
- bowl
- spoon

CARVE YOUR OWN
SOAP ART

What do you like to do? Do you like to dance, play soccer, or climb trees? Do you have a favorite pet? Create a petroglyph in a bar of soap to represent your interests. Or, you can just make some fun designs like the simple geometric shapes Native Americans sometimes carved.

1 Place your bar of soap on a workspace covered in newspaper.

2 Once you decide what you would like to carve, draw an outline of the image into the soap using your pencil.

3 Using the plastic knife, carve or chip away the soap around your outline until you are left with your basic shape. Scrape away small bits at a time so the soap doesn't break into chunks.

4 Finish your design by using the toothpick to add details inside the outline.

5 Wet your finger and rub it over the surface of the soap to create a smooth finish. Just don't wipe all your details off!

6 Let your petroglyph dry and harden for a full day before handling it.

SUPPLIES

- bar of soap
- newspaper
- pencil
- plastic knife
- toothpick
- water

CHAPTER 2

The Archaic and Formative Periods

omething happened around 8000 **BCE** that would change the lives of Native Americans forever. The large animals of the Americas began to die off. The woolly mammoths, saber-toothed tigers, mastodons, and giant armadillos all became extinct. The countless numbers of massive animals roaming the land were gone.

Why did this happen? Scientists aren't exactly sure, but most believe that the melting of the North American **glaciers** caused the **climate** to change. According to this theory, significantly warmer temperatures killed trees and plants that could not adapt quickly.

With fewer plants to eat, smaller animals would have died soon afterward. And with fewer smaller animals to eat, the larger animals would have also died. Extinction worked its way right up the **food chain**.

Without large animals to hunt, Native Americans had to find other sources of food.

This started a shift from the **nomadic** hunting lifestyle of the **Archaic Period** to a more **agricultural** lifestyle in permanent settlements in the **Formative Period**. And it was during the Formative Period that Native American cultures began to flourish in new ways. With more free time, people became interested in things they'd never even imagined when hunting and gathering food was their only priority.

WORDS TO KNOW

BCE: put after a date, BCE stands for Before Common Era and counts down to zero. CE stands for Common Era and counts up from zero. These non-religious terms correspond to BC and AD.

glacier: a huge mass of ice and snow.

climate: the average weather patterns in an area over a long period of time.

food chain: a community of animals and plants where each different plant or animal is eaten by another plant or animal higher up in the chain.

nomadic: moving from place to place to find food.

Archaic Period: the name given by archaeologists to the earliest periods of a culture.

agricultural: based on farming.

Formative Period: a period defined by the development of agriculture, the establishment of permanent settlements, and the development of the arts.

Glaciers are still melting today. When Glacier National Park in Montana was established in 1910, it contained about 150 glaciers. A survey of the park in 2010 revealed only 25 glaciers.

PLANTS AND POTTERY

As early as 5000 BCE, about 3,000 years after the great animal die-off, Native Americans in what is now Mexico were collecting and planting corn kernels to grow **maize**. About 1,500 years later, around 3500 BCE, they began **cultivating** squash, beans, and potatoes.

Because of their agricultural lifestyle, Native Americans lived in seasonal villages and developed new tools to grow and cook the food they farmed. Every day, women ground seeds and corn into **meal** using stone tools called metates and manos. Adding water to the ground meal formed a paste like pancake batter, which they cooked over a fire on a stone griddle.

WORDS TO KNOW

maize: corn.

cultivate: to prepare and use land for growing food.

meal: the edible part of a grain, ground into a powder such as cornmeal.

traditional: a belief, custom, or way of doing things that has been passed on from generation to generation for a long time.

DID YOU KNOW?

Today, blenders and milling machines have replaced metates and manos. Only a few remote cultures, including the Tarahumara of Mexico, still use these **traditional** tools.

Native Americans soon began making pottery to store seeds and kernels to use later.

They also figured out how to use stones to boil water inside clay pots for cooking plants, roots, and corn. By heating stones over a fire to very hot temperatures and scooping them into a pot, they could get the water in the pot warm enough to boil. Why didn't they just hang the pot over the fire? Their pots probably weren't strong enough to withstand an open flame.

The Atlatl

The Native Americans who lived around 3500 BCE were not just improving their farming and cooking skills. They were improving their hunting tools as well, even though hunting was no longer the sole focus of their life. Caribou, moose, elk, bears, and other animals roaming North America were good sources of food, blankets, clothing, and tools. Native Americans hadn't yet invented the bow and arrow, but they had a type of spear thrower called the atlatl. The atlatl was a thick stick or bone with a hook on the end that hunters used to increase the throwing distance of a spear. They held on to the atlatl as they whipped the spear, called a dart or yaomitl, at the target. Explorers from Europe saw atlatls being used in the 1500s in modern-day Mexico, and the tool certainly existed in the Americas long before that. There is also evidence of atlatls in Africa 25,000 years ago.

EARTHWORKS

Imagine a giant, serpent-shaped mound 5 feet tall (1½ meters), 20 feet wide (6 meters), and ¼ mile long (0.4 kilometers). What could it represent? No one knows the true meaning of Serpent Mound. Some scientists think the southern Ohio mound may represent a sacred calendar or an eclipse, and others connect it to cycles of birth, death, and nature.

Serpent Mound is just one of more than 11,000 gigantic earthwork mounds built by the Adena people who lived in what is now Ohio, Pennsylvania, and southern New York.

Another mound was 68 feet high (21 meters), nearly seven stories tall! Through carbon-14 testing, scientists believe that this work was done around 1000 BCE. It's hard to imagine how people moved so much dirt with only their hands and wooden shovels. Today we would use heavy construction equipment.

DID YOU KNOW?
In 2000, builders working on a neighborhood of new homes at a construction site in California unearthed centuries-old human remains, including 50 complete skeletons. Members of the Miwok and Ohlone tribes lived in the area between 1000 and 1400 CE.

Archaeologists have also uncovered Native American burial grounds throughout North America. They have found bodies smeared with red pigment buried with objects such as arrowheads, tools, and jewelry. In 1883, archaeologists excavated Criel Mound in West Virginia. They uncovered bodies buried at different depths in the mound, including an Adena leader in the center and 10 of his servants circled around him.

THE OLMECS:
THEIR SCULPTURES AND ARTISANS

Also around 1000 BCE, Native Americans living far to the south in southeast Mexico began to build large-scale stoneworks. These people, known as the Olmecs, constructed pyramids with temples and sometimes even palaces at the top. They carved large stone sculptures, such as 18-ton heads, without the use of wheels or iron tools. They also made sculptures of serpents in the same shape as the mounds built by the Adena people. Their massive sculptures and monuments influenced all the civilizations that lived in the region after them. The fact that these structures were so large and took so much thought and effort to build is evidence that these early communities were becoming permanent.

The relics left behind by the Olmec civilization show that members of this society had specialized jobs.

Some were craftspeople, others were farmers, and still others were workers who hauled stones from miles away. This type of organization would only have occurred in a permanent settlement. Why? If people were on the move hunting animals, they wouldn't have the time or the need for these types of jobs.

WORDS TO KNOW

artisan: a skilled worker who makes things by hand.

magnetite: a type of iron ore in which you can sometimes see your reflection.

inlaid: when one material is set into the surface of another material to create a design.

semiprecious: minerals that can be used as gems but are considered less valuable than precious stones.

Mesoamerica: the region that includes parts of Mexico and Central America.

Olmec **artisans** figured out how to use a shiny material called **magnetite** to create basic mirrors. For the first time, people could see their own reflections clearly without looking into a river or stream. This discovery may have contributed to the face-painting and jewelry-wearing trends in the region, since people could see how they looked with their faces and bodies decorated. These trends became so popular that priests and wealthy people even began to have their teeth **inlaid** with shiny, **semiprecious** stones.

MAYA AT PLAY

By about 500 CE, the Maya civilization was thriving in the area now known as **Mesoamerica**. This is a region of about 125,000 square miles (300,000 square kilometers), including what is now Southern Mexico and the countries of Belize, Guatemala, El Salvador, and Honduras.

There is much evidence that the Maya played games. You might think playing games is just something people have always done for fun. But imagine you're one of the earliest Native Americans who had to hunt mastodons just to survive. You would be too busy to ever dream of kicking a ball around with your friends.

One of the most well-known Maya games was a fast and furious ball game called Pok-A-Tok. In every major Maya city, men played Pok-A-Tok on sunken courts. Two teams tried to put a 6-pound, hard rubbery ball (almost 3 kilograms) through a stone hoop as high as 20 feet off the ground (6 meters). Players could only use their head, shoulders, elbows, wrists, and hips to move the ball and the game ended when someone finally got the ball through the ring. This could take days!

WORDS TO KNOW

sacrifice: to kill a person or animal as an offering to a god.

DID YOU KNOW?

For the Maya, Pok-A-Tok symbolized the struggle of life over death. The losing team was often *sacrificed* to the gods, while the winners were given a feast.

Maya Beauty

The Maya traded with other societies for things like honey, cocoa, shells, and cotton cloth. And they began to fashion the things they acquired, as well as their own bodies, into works of art. They considered crossed eyes to be very beautiful, so mothers often hung beads between their babies' eyes to help pull their pupils inward. They also admired flat, long foreheads, so mothers strapped boards to their babies' heads to make their foreheads grow long and slanted. Older children had their adult teeth filed to a point or a T-shape and decorated with stones of jade, obsidian, or hematite. This may all sound strange, but the Maya would have found us just as odd for dyeing our hair different colors and wearing high-heeled shoes.

CULTURES EVOLVE

By the time explorers like Christopher Columbus and Hernando de Soto began to arrive in North America from Europe in the 1400s and 1500s, there were hundreds of Native American cultures throughout the continent. These cultures had their own unique customs and ways of life adapted to their environments and the available natural resources. Members of the Anasazi culture in the Southwest were so skilled at basket weaving that their baskets could hold water. That's something that most modern, machine-made baskets cannot do!

Tribes along the coasts, for example, were experts at fishing in the ocean, while inland tribes were expert hunters. Tribes that lived far to the north built igloos using the snow around them, while those in the dry desert lands of the Southwest and Mexico were skilled at building homes of clay.

To help you understand these cultures and their development, this book explores six major Native American cultural regions of North America. The chapters that follow will explain what life was like for the people of the Northeast Woodlands and Great Lakes, Southeast, Great Plains, Southwest and Mesoamerica, Pacific Northwest, and Arctic.

BUILD YOUR OWN
ARCHAIC TOOLKIT

Native Americans who lived during the Archaic Period had to create tools out of things they found in nature. You can do the same thing. Imagine you have no pots, pans, pencils, knives, or containers. Go out into your backyard or to a local park and gather things you might be able to use as tools. Think carefully about how you might use everything you find. That's what Native Americans had to do in order to survive.

You might find some sticks that are good for digging and others that are good for spearing. Some rocks are good for hammering and others are good for scraping against other rocks like chalk on a blackboard. You might find leaves that are thick and bushy to stuff a pillow and leaves that are waxy and strong enough to hold things when they are tied together, like a small basket.

Now try using your tools in different ways. How will you carry and store water? How can your tools help you to eat food? What kind of shelter do you need? How can you carry things from place to place.

See how many Archaic tools you can find near your own house, and then look for more the next time you take a trip somewhere else. You'll see that different areas have different kinds of rocks, sticks, and leaves, and that each of them can be used for different things. What else can you find?

CHAPTER 3

The Northeast Woodlands and Great Lakes Tribes
ALGONQUIAN & IROQUOIS

hen the earliest Native Americans lived between present-day Boston and Detroit, the territory was a vast woodland full of trees and animals. It stretched north up into New York state and Maine, south to New Jersey, Delaware, and Maryland, and west through Pennsylvania to the Ohio Valley. There, it connected with the Great Lakes.

With great forests covering this land, the Native Americans in the region relied on trees for many basic needs. From just the bark of a tree, they made walls for their homes, food and water containers, eating trays, canoe skins, and even woven nets. Tree roots were used like rope to tie things together, while the wood of the tree itself was turned into things like spears, arrows, canoes, and snowshoes.

When the European explorers arrived, they discovered that Native Americans had already developed axes to cut down trees and **adzes** to shape pieces of wood. They had also created **gouges**, which they used like our modern-day **chisels** to hollow out tree trunks to make canoes for transportation.

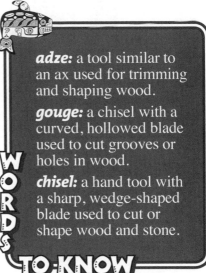

WORDS TO KNOW

adze: a tool similar to an ax used for trimming and shaping wood.

gouge: a chisel with a curved, hollowed blade used to cut grooves or holes in wood.

chisel: a hand tool with a sharp, wedge-shaped blade used to cut or shape wood and stone.

CLIMATE AND SHELTER

Ever since North American glaciers began melting around 10,000 years ago, the climate in this area has been similar to today, with hot summers, cold winters, and moderate temperatures in the fall and spring. Although Native Americans found ways to survive everywhere in the Americas, this region's temperatures were more comfortable to live in than some others, like the Arctic Circle.

❁ People could take advantage of the seasons, growing enough **crops** and hunting enough game during the spring, summer, and fall to last through the winter.

Archaeologists have discovered permanent settlements among Native Americans who farmed in the Ohio Valley, such as the Monongahela tribe. They built small oval or circular houses with wooden posts and **thatched** roofs. Their large villages surrounded by **palisades** were well organized and included up to several hundred people. Other tribes, such as the Iroquois in New York, lived in **longhouses** built for up to 20 extended families to live together.

WORDS TO KNOW

crop: a plant grown for food and other uses.

thatch: straw, leaves, or any similar material used for making a roof.

palisade: a fence made of rows of pointed posts.

longhouse: the traditional building that housed several Iroquois families.

wigwam: the rounded or rectangular home of the Algonquian tribes.

sapling: a young tree.

East of the Ohio Valley, Native Americans hunted and lived in dome or cone-shaped **wigwams** made of bark stretched over a frame made from **saplings**. These structures could hold up in all weather conditions. Some only had enough space for two people and others could fit up to eight family members.

Life in a Longhouse

The Iroquois called themselves the Haudenosaunee, or "People of the Longhouse." Their houses were sometimes 150 feet long (46 meters) and as many as 60 family members might live together in one longhouse. A path ran the length of the longhouse, and curtains hung on either side of the path to allow each family a small amount of privacy. The curtains, like the longhouse door, were made of animal skins, and each private area was no bigger than 54 square feet (5 square meters). That's about the size of a modern-day bathroom—and it was the private area for a mother, father, and their children!

The oldest woman was put in charge of the longhouse since the men were off hunting for long periods of time. Except for the hunting tools and clothes of the men, she was considered the owner of everything in the longhouse. Women oversaw all the daily chores and duties, from food preparation and the sewing of clothing to making sponges out of corncobs and helping their daughters sew together dolls using *corn silk* for doll's hair.

The Iroquois originally built their villages next to rivers for easy access to water, but later they settled on hilltops for protection from other tribes.

WORDS TO KNOW

corn silk: the long, silky fibers that hang out of a corn husk.

NEIGHBORING LANGUAGE FAMILIES

The Iroquois were a **confederacy** of tribes united by a common language called Iroquoian. The Iroquois tribes included the Mohawk, Oneida, Onondaga, Cayuga, Seneca, and Tuscarora. They lived all over upper New York state, the St. Lawrence Valley, and the shores of Lakes Erie and Ontario.

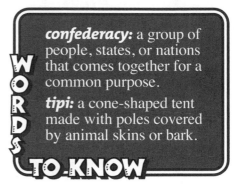

WORDS TO KNOW

confederacy: a group of people, states, or nations that comes together for a common purpose.

tipi: a cone-shaped tent made with poles covered by animal skins or bark.

DID YOU KNOW?

Cone-shaped wigwams are different from the **tipis** used by Native Americans of the Great Plains. Wigwams cannot be packed up and moved like tipis. And only tipis have smoke flaps and a top opening for cooking inside.

The Algonquians were a group of many tribes as well. They lived to the east, west, north, and south of the Iroquois tribes, from Maine to the Great Lakes area and from Canada to the middle Atlantic region. The Algonquians were also linked by language and included the Abenakis in Maine, Mohegans in Long Island and Connecticut, Wampanoags in Massachusetts, Shawnees in the Ohio Valley, Powhatans in Virginia, Lenni Lenape in New Jersey and Delaware, and Nanticokes in Delaware and Maryland. Maybe you have also heard of the Arapahos, Narragansetts, Chippewas, and Penobscots.

Historians believe there were about 500,000 Native Americans in the Northeast Woodlands in the 1300s and 1400s. Most were members of either the Iroquois or Algonquian language families.

Algonquian languages were spoken across much of North America, similar to how English is spoken throughout the United States today. Some Algonquian words even made their way into the English language. Algonquian gave tribes from different places a way to communicate with one another, just as people today from Texas, Massachusetts, and England are all able to communicate in English.

Speaking Algonquian

• •

Algonquian is not just one language, but a group of related languages. These were widely spoken in North America before the European explorers arrived. Today, Americans still use about many Algonquian words, including many names of places. Massachusetts and Connecticut are two states with Algonquian names and there are many towns and rivers and mountains, such as Natick, Chappaquiddick, Cohasset and Annisquam. How many can you think of?

See how many sentences you can create using these Algonquian words:

caribou	papoose	terrapin
chipmunk	pecan	toboggan
hickory	raccoon	tomahawk
hominy	skunk	totem
moccasin	squash	wigwam
moose	succotash	woodchuck

FOOD

The Algonquian and Iroquois people grew corn, tobacco, and other crops, but they also hunted for food. The hunting methods of this period were far more advanced than those of the earliest Native Americans. People who lived during these later years could sometimes hunt and catch more food than they actually needed.

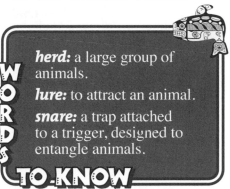

WORDS TO KNOW

herd: a large group of animals.

lure: to attract an animal.

snare: a trap attached to a trigger, designed to entangle animals.

One animal found in great quantities in the Northeast Woodlands was moose. Because moose do not live in **herds**, they have to be hunted one at a time. Hunters in this region invented several clever tools to **lure** moose into their traps. They made whistle-like instruments from birchbark that made a sound similar to the moose's mating call. They used it to draw a moose toward an overhead **snare** hung from tree branches. When the moose stepped onto a branch connected to the trap, a net fell and caught the animal.

In the Great Lakes area, many Native Americans became experts at fishing, too. They learned that some fish were attracted to light. So they strapped torches onto their canoes, paddled out onto the lake at night, and waited with spears for the fish to swim toward the light.

Without refrigerators or freezers to store **surplus** food, people had to find a way to **preserve** it. Archaeologists have discovered evidence that Native Americans of the Eastern Woodlands used smoke to preserve their food and then stored it in **silos**, much like modern-day farmers store corn, wheat, and other crops. Native American silos were deep holes lined with marsh grass and covered with bark to keep out animals and the weather.

surplus: extra; more than what is needed.

preserve: to keep fresh or safe.

silo: an airtight pit or tower in which food can be stored.

WORDS TO KNOW

CLOTHING AND JEWELRY

Appearance was important to Native Americans living in the Eastern Woodlands and Great Lakes regions during the 1300s and 1400s. In the Great Lakes region, people dug up copper and became experts at shaping it into earrings, nose rings, and other forms of jewelry. To make jewelry and other copper items like fishhooks, blades, and

drills, they pounded a nugget of copper into a thin sheet, like a rolled-out piece of dough. Then they used a sharp point to outline the shape they wanted. Next, they cracked the sheet until the outlined item popped out.

Scientists have found copper items made in this way from the Great Lakes to as far east as New York state.

The Iroquois are known to have carved hair combs out of animal bones. Some Native Americans used mussel shells found along the Atlantic coast or Great Lakes shores as tweezers to pluck out unwanted hair. People also used the shells they collected to make jewelry or **wampum**.

What is Wampum?

The word *wampum* comes from the Narragansett word for "white shell beads." Wampum was either white, made from **whelk** shells, or purple-black, made from **quahog** shells. Different colors and designs of wampum had different meanings. A purple background inside in a white border, for instance, sometimes indicated a once-unfriendly relationship turned peaceful. Wampum belts that were painted red were a call to war. Native Americans searched the beaches of present-day New Jersey and Long Island for whelk shells, which were the most common shells used for wampum. They poked holes in these shells and then strung them together into long belts that were used as decoration and to tell stories.

Europeans arrived in the 1400s and 1500s—many decades after the Native Americans began creating wampum. Wampum evolved from a decoration and form of communication into a form of **currency**. It was more plentiful than metal coins, so European explorers began to trade wampum for goods and services, just as they would have traded coins if they had enough of them to pass around in the New World. Purple wampum was twice as valuable as the white beads because there were far more whelk than quahog shells on the beaches.

WARRING TRIBES AND IDEAS OF PEACE

As the Algonquian and Iroquois tribes grew, they began to hunt each other's animals and get more and more in each other's way. Some people were willing to fight to keep what they believed was their territory.

The Iroquois rose to prominence in the 1300s. They dominated the Algonquian tribes, as well as all the Native American tribes living between New England and the Mississippi River and from Ontario down to Tennessee. They used spears, knives, rocks, and tomahawks when they went to war.

All this violence bothered a man named Deganawidah, who had a vision of uniting the many tribes. Around 1570, one of his followers, named Hiawatha, convinced the Seneca, Cayuga, Onondaga, Oneida, and Mohawk tribes to stop fighting and accept the Great Law of Peace. Leaders from each tribe came together to form the Five Nations, known as the Iroquois Confederacy. Instead of fighting each other they worked together.

The Five Nations became one of the most powerful groups in North America. This helped them when the Europeans began trying to take control of their land, because they stood together in resistance. A sixth tribe, the Tuscarora, joined in the 1700s.

DID YOU KNOW?

Wampum belts tell some of the story of the Iroquois Confederacy using strings of colored beads. The Hiawatha Belt is a strand of 892 white and 5,682 purple beads showing the five original members of the Iroquois Confederacy as squares on either side of a tree.

CREATE YOUR OWN
ALGONQUIAN ART

Much of what we know about the Algonquian people comes from pictographs and petroglyphs. These are two styles of artwork that many Native American tribes produced. Pictographs are paintings done on bark, while petroglyphs are images carved onto stone. You can practice both kinds of artwork.

1 If you can't find a large piece of bark, use a piece of paper to make a pictograph. Paint a common scene from your daily life. For instance, you might create a scene that shows your family having dinner together at the kitchen table or you and your friends playing soccer for your school team.

SUPPLIES

- large piece of bark or piece of paper
- paint and paintbrushes
- small rock
- large rock with a flat surface

2 To make a petroglyph, use the small rock to scratch out a scene on the large rock. Do you want to create the same scene or something different?

3 When you've completed both the pictograph and the petroglyph, compare them. Which is clearer? Which is more detailed? Was one form of art harder to do than the other? Which do you prefer? Which do you think will last longer, the bark painting or the rock carving?

CHAPTER 4

The Southeast Tribes
CHEROKEE, CATAWBA, CREEK & SEMINOLE

The region that makes up what is today Virginia, North and South Carolina, Georgia, Florida, and Alabama is much different from that of the Northeast Woodlands. It is defined by forests, swamps, and the vast Appalachian Mountain range that covers much of the area.

Many of the southern Appalachian peaks are between 2,000 and 4,000 feet high (610–1,220 meters), but in North Carolina, Mount Mitchell rises to a whopping 6,684 feet (2,037 meters). Many rivers wind their way down the mountainsides to sea level and eventually find their way to the Atlantic Ocean.

The lifestyles of the tribes in this region depended on the location of their villages. Life in the mountains was much different than life along the Atlantic coast. Inland tribes focused on farming while those along the coast became experts at fishing. The temperature ranges in the Appalachian Mountain region are wide, with frigid winter nights on the mountain peaks and hot summer afternoons just inland of the coast.

CHEROKEE FARMERS

About 50,000 Cherokees controlled much of the Carolinas, Georgia, and Alabama by the mid-1600s. They lived in at least 200 villages, some of them stretching into parts of Virginia, Tennessee, and Kentucky. Each member of the Cherokee tribe belonged to one of seven clans, which are groups of families that are related. Cherokee society was matrilineal, which means children automatically became members of their mother's clan at birth.

Even among traditional Cherokee today, all clan members are considered brothers and sisters, so it is forbidden for them to marry someone from their own clan.

The Cherokee were farmers who stayed in their villages year-round. Did their settled lifestyle influence the houses they lived in? They built strong, permanent structures they called *asi*. These homes are like upside-down baskets made of tree branches covered with plaster and thatch. A typical village could have as many as 60 of these homes.

foundation: the base of a home that is partly underground and supports the weight of the building.

insulate: to keep the heat in and the cold out.

wattle and daub: a type of house construction made by weaving a frame of river cane, wood, and vines that is coated with a mud plaster and a thatch or bark roof.

Each *asi* was built on a large, round hole dug into the ground, similar to the cement **foundations** built into the ground for houses today. Like the circular houses of the Algonquian tribes, the underground section of the house was warm during the winter and cool in summer. It was a comfortable place to sleep, and the dirt floor was a perfect place to build a fire for cooking.

To further **insulate** their homes, the Cherokee spread a layer of mud over the branches that formed their aboveground walls and roof. This technique is called **wattle and daub**. The wattle is the frame of branches and the daub is the mud packed on top of the wattle. Building their homes small and low made it easier to keep them warm in winter.

✹✹ Some Cherokee actually built larger, rectangular summer homes that fit larger extended families, and then lived in their *asi* only in winter.

Each home had a single doorway, plus a hole in the roof to let smoke escape when a fire was burning inside for cooking or heating. Eventually the Cherokee built their homes using thick logs instead of thin branches, which made them stronger and more like log cabins than thatched huts. Mud was used to fill in the cracks between the logs.

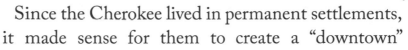

Since the Cherokee lived in permanent settlements, it made sense for them to create a "downtown" area where villagers could get together and discuss matters that were important to the community. These meeting places were **heptagonal** structures called council houses. The shape gave **representatives** of the Bird, Paint, Deer, Wolf, Blue, Long Hair, and Wild Potato clans each a section of seats around a **sacred** fire.

WORDS TO KNOW

heptagonal: something with seven sides.

representative: a single person who speaks for the wishes of a group.

sacred: highly valued and important.

GROWING POPULATIONS CAUSE FRICTION

The Cherokee were the biggest and most dominant tribe in the Southeast, but they were not the only one. There were also the Catawba and the Creek, as well as the Chickasaw, Shawnee, and Choctaw. As the Cherokee Nation grew and spread throughout the Southeast, it fought with the Catawba and the Creek, especially in the mid-1700s. After several years of fighting, the Cherokee forced the Catawba and Creek farther inland and out of their way.

DID YOU KNOW?

Cherokee log homes were very much like the log cabins people build today, but instead of having smoke holes in our roofs, now we have brick or stone fireplaces connected to chimneys.

The Catawba, meaning "river people," lived along the Catawba River in the area that is now North and South Carolina.

Sequoyah's Talking Leaves

One of the most famous Cherokee was a man named Sequoyah, who invented a written language. Sequoyah spoke several languages. As European **settlers** moved closer to Cherokee lands, Sequoyah noticed them communicating using marks on paper, which he called talking leaves because the paper seemed to talk to the reader.

Sequoyah worried that, since their language was only spoken, Cherokee children would start speaking and writing in English and forget their own culture. He wanted a written language so that his people could preserve their own **heritage**. Beginning in 1809, Sequoyah set to work on a written alphabet. Some people made fun of Sequoyah's work and even set his cabin on fire to destroy his papers. But in 1821, Sequoyah finished his **syllabary** of 86 symbols, which represented all the syllables in the Cherokee language. The Cherokee became the first group of Native Americans to develop a written language. By 1828, thousands of Cherokee were using their written language on a daily basis and the first Native American newspaper, called the *Cherokee Phoenix*, was published in both Cherokee and English.

WORDS TO KNOW

settler: a person who is one of the first to live in an area.

heritage: a culture passed down through generations.

syllabary: a set of characters representing syllables that is used like an alphabet.

Catawba were fierce warriors who believed in looking as bold as they acted. They used face paint to frighten their enemies, painting their faces black with a white circle around one eye and a black circle around the other. Like the Maya, they used boards to flatten the foreheads of baby boys so that as adult warriors their face paint would stand out more.

The Creek also fought the Cherokee. Like the Cherokee, the Creek lived in permanent towns, which they called *italwa*, with smaller villages around it called *talofas*. Plazas in the towns contained a **rotunda**, made of poles and mud and used for council meetings, and an open-air summer council house.

WORDS TO-KNOW

rotunda: a round structure.

DID YOU KNOW?

Most communities today have at least one building that brings people together, much like a council house. Your town hall, post office, and school are all gathering places for members of your city or town.

Once an *italwa* reached between 400 and 600 people, about half the population moved to start a new *italwa* with its own villages. This spread the Creek way of life and kept the *italwa* from becoming overpopulated. Members of one town often visited other *italwas* and *talofas* to stay connected with family and friends.

By the 1700s, the Creeks were becoming more spread out as they grew more and more crops. Some of their homes were separated by over a mile or more of corn, rice, or potatoes.

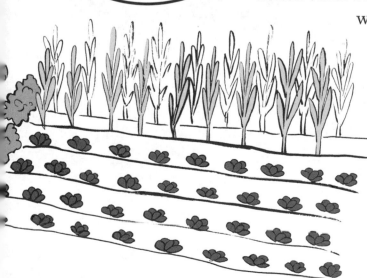

> Women started using plows and axes to help ease the burden of tending their crops by hand.

Because the lifestyle of the Creek required a lot of land, their society began to clash with the Cherokee. Both societies were growing and there wasn't always enough land between their settlements for hunting. Unfortunately for the Creek and Catawba, there were simply too many Cherokee for them to overcome. The Cherokee dominated the area into the 1800s, when the newborn United States of America began removing the Cherokee from their land and giving it to settlers.

PEOPLE ON THE MOVE

Another Southeastern tribe whose name is widely known today is the Seminole. The Seminoles were **descendants** of the Creeks. They moved south to flee fighting with Cherokee tribes and United States **troops**. In the empty swampland of southern Florida, the Seminoles were left alone. Farmers weren't interested in the land, so no one was fighting over it.

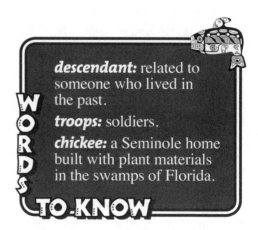

WORDS TO KNOW

descendant: related to someone who lived in the past.

troops: soldiers.

chickee: a Seminole home built with plant materials in the swamps of Florida.

To survive in the swamps, the Seminoles created **chickee** huts. A chickee was an open-air thatched hut that could be constructed in a single day. *Chickee* means "house" in the Seminole language. Chickee huts were built on stilts high above swampy waters. They had platforms of split logs and roofs of palmetto leaves.

The name *Seminole* actually means "wild people" or "runaway." In this case, running away or **retreating** was a tool of survival. At a time when Native Americans and settlers were fighting in the Carolinas and Georgia, these peaceful people probably would have been killed if they had stayed behind. Moving south helped them to preserve their culture, which continues today.

WORDS TO-KNOW

retreat: to move away from danger.

mascot: a symbol of an organization.

Florida State Seminoles

Seminoles are the symbol for Florida State University. Students paint their faces before important sporting events similar to the way Native Americans did before battle. This tradition is upsetting to some Native Americans because they feel it makes fun of their ancestors. As a result, many colleges and universities have stopped using Native American **mascots.** Stanford University, for example, changed from the Indian to the Cardinal, which is the school color. But the Seminole Tribe of Florida has worked with Florida State University to plan specific traditions that open the school's home football games. They even give traditional clothing to a student to wear as he or she enters the stadium on a horse and plants a flaming spear at midfield.

SYLLABARY PRACTICE

Have you ever learned a completely new language? Try using the Cherokee syllabary developed by Sequoyah to write out some Cherokee words. With enough practice, you could be writing in Cherokee in no time! Here are some words and their meanings for you to work with. They are broken into syllables for you.

- Sequoyah
- Tsalagi *(Cherokee)*
- o-si-yo *(hello)*
- u-ni-tsi *(mother)*
- a-da-do-da *(father)*
- di-na-da-nv-tli *(brother)*
- u-lv *(sister)*
- a-tsa-di *(fish)*
- S-v-no-yi-e-hi-nv-do *(moon)*
- a-wi-yu-s-ti *(antelope)*
- u-s-di *(baby)*
- u-wo-du-hi *(beautiful)*
- a-da-le-s-gi-yi-s-gi *(monkey)*
- su-na-le-i *(morning)*
- ma-ma *(salt)*
- ka-no-gi-s-di *(song)*

D a		R e	T i	Ꮟ o	Ꮕ u	i v
S ga Ꮜ ka		Ꮞ ge	Y gi	A go	J gu	E gv
Ꮀ ha		P he	Ꮧ hi	Ꮂ ho	Ꮁ hu	Ꮕ hv
W la		Ꮣ le	P li	G lo	M lu	Ꮜ lv
Ꮉ ma		Ꮊ me	H mi	Ꮬ mo	Y mu	
Ꮎ na Ꮕ hna Ꮹ nah		Ꮑ ne	Ꮒ ni	Z no	Ꮖ nu	Ꮗ nv
Ꮐ qua		Ꮙ que	Ꮝ qui	Ꮗ quo	Ꮜ quv	Ꭼ quv
Ꮝ s Ꮎ sa		Ꮞ se	Ꮟ si	Ꮠ so	Ꮡ su	R sv
Ꮣ da Ꮤ ta		Ꮥ de Ꮦ te	Ꮧ di Ꮨ ti	V do	S du	Ꮛ dv
Ꮤ dla Ꮣ tla		L tle	C tli	Ꮭ tlo	Ꮰ tlu	P tlv
G tsa		V tse	Ꮳ tsi	K tso	Ꮫ tsu	Ꮷ tsv
Ꮹ wa		Ꮳ we	Ꮻ wi	Ꮽ wo	Ꮾ wv	Ꮿ wv
Ꮿ ya		B ye	Ꮵ yi	Ꮠ yo	Ꮉ yv	B yv

TRY THIS

Use your new skills to write a story in Cherokee. You can look up words at http://cherokee.org/AboutTheNation/Wordlist.aspx

Just type in a word in English and press search. The site will give you the word in Cherokee.

PRACTICE WITH
FACE PAINT DESIGNS

Face painting is an ancient tradition for many Native Americans cultures and it is still used today in religious ceremonies. Traditionally, Native Americans made face paint out of berries, roots, dirt, and plants. Today's face paints come in many colors that can be applied safely to the skin. Explore the colors and patterns used by different Native American tribes and try painting the face of a friend or classmate. Were there different designs for boys and girls? You can also make up your own designs to represent something important in your own life. Ask an adult to supervise if you use the Internet.

1 Research traditional Native American face paint designs and choose one or create your own.

2 Find a friend or classmate who is willing to have you practice on him or her.

3 If you are starting with a base color that covers the face, use a make-up sponge to apply it. Use smaller brushes for detailed designs and for the corners around the eyes and mouth.

4 Use a damp paper towel to wipe away mistakes.

5 Take a picture of the design you have made before your friend washes it off!

SUPPLIES

- books on Native Americans or Internet access
- friend or classmate
- face paint
- make-up sponge
- small make-up brushes or paintbrushes
- paper towels
- water
- camera

TRY THIS

Try making your own face paint. You can mix cornstarch and water into a paste and then add food coloring until you have a color you like. You can also try a mixture of light corn syrup and flour.

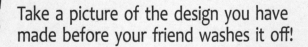

CHAPTER 5

The Great Plains Tribes
THE CHEYENNE, LAKOTA SIOUX & COMANCHE

The Great Plains region of North America stretches far and wide, from Canada all the way down through North and South Dakota, Nebraska, Kansas, Oklahoma, and Northern Texas. It covers the land from the Mississippi River as far west as the Rocky Mountains. This is a dry expanse of flat land and rolling hills covered in tall grasses.

This land offered excellent **grazing** for the enormous herds of **bison** that roamed the region. The people who lived in the Great Plains moved with the animals, hunting them along the way as their main source of food.

ON THE GO—BY FOOT

Can you imagine packing up your house and all of your belongings every couple of months and moving everything to a new place? The Native Americans in this part of the continent invented tools to make the moving process easier. The Cheyenne and Lakota Sioux tribes used a **travois** pulled by dogs to move their belongings.

WORDS TO KNOW

graze: to eat grass.

bison: the correct name for an animal called the buffalo.

travois: a sled consisting of a net or platform dragged along the ground between two poles that are pulled by a horse or dog.

Travois were made of two long poles connected with material similar to a net. One end of each pole was attached to the dogs' shoulders, and the other end simply dragged on the ground behind the dog as it walked. When it was time to move, the Native Americans loaded the travois with supplies. They walked along while the dogs pulled loads of up to 250 pounds (over 110 kilograms).

The people of the Great Plains needed tools they could carry easily and use in many ways again and again. The travois was a multipurpose tool. Once a group arrived at its new camp, they used the long poles of the travois to build fences to trap buffalo and to create frames for tipis.

THE ALL-IMPORTANT BUFFALO

The people of the Great Plains naturally relied on buffalo meat for food. Women mixed dried bison meat, berries, and animal fat into cakes called pemmican that kept for years. It was like a buffalo meat version of an energy bar!

No part of the buffalo was wasted. **Hides** were used to make cradles for newborn babies, curtains, tipi walls, clothing, blankets, and even canvases for painting pictures. Buffalo hair was woven into rope or used to stuff pillows, **moccasins**, and gloves. Horns and bones were carved into spoons, cups, knives, and **awls**, while the largest bones, like the ribs, were made into small sleds. What about the hooves? They made great rattles for children. Buffalo stomachs made useful cooking pots and the tails made excellent flyswatters!

MOCCASIN

hide: the skin of an animal.

moccasin: a shoe made of soft, flexible leather or animal skin.

awl: a small, pointed tool used to make holes, especially in leather.

WORDS TO KNOW

BUFFALO TAIL FLY SWATTER

HOOF BABY RATTLE

ON THE GO—ON HORSEBACK

Nobody is exactly sure when the first horses arrived in the Americas, but the animals were likely here by the 1500s. We do know that when Europeans began to explore the continent they brought horses with them. Some of these horses ran away to the Great Plains, but most horses came to the area through trade.

The Native Americans living on the Plains soon discovered how much horses could help them.

The Buffalo Jump

A herd of buffalo can run up to 30 miles per hour (50 kilometers per hour) and until the Spanish explorers came with horses in the 1500s, Native Americans hunted buffalo on foot. Do you think this was dangerous? Buffalo have poor eyesight and are very large animals traveling in groups of up to 50. In areas where there were cliffs, a group of hunters chased a herd of buffalo toward a cliff while another group shouted and forced them over the edge. Hunters waiting below killed the injured buffalo after they jumped. This hunting method became known as the "buffalo jump."

Because horses were much bigger and stronger than dogs, the Native Americans of the Great Plains were able to use a larger travois pulled by a horse as they migrated with the buffalo herds. This helped the Plains people to carry more supplies on hunts. Infants and small children could ride on the bigger travois, making the journey easier for their parents.

Horses also allowed Native Americans to cover more ground. On foot, people can't keep up with buffalo, but on horseback, they could steer the animals where they wanted them to go. When tribes from the East and European settlers started making their way inland to the Great Plains region, fighting resulted over territory and hunting rights. Horses became an important tool of war.

COMANCHE HORSES IN BATTLE

The Comanche living in the southern Plains became the most expert horsemen in all of the Americas. They prized their horses the way someone today might value an expensive car. But they also considered their horses loyal friends. Owning several horses was a sign of wealth and it wasn't uncommon for a Comanche warrior to own over 1,000 horses. They chose the strongest, fastest horses possible. One Comanche tribe of 2,000 people is said to have owned more than 15,000 horses.

Before going into battle, a Comanche warrior put war paint on his own face and on his horse's face.

The horse was the Comanche's partner in battle, not just a tool of transportation. Warriors practiced riding their horses for hours and hours, day after day, perfecting stunts and movements that would help them in battle. When a fellow warrior was injured on the ground, a Comanche would ride quickly to him and scoop him up with one arm without even slowing down! This was a move they practiced a lot, and it helped save many lives.

The Sideways Maneuver

The Comanche developed a technique called the sideways maneuver that let them ride their horses with no hands. A warrior strapped a sling made of buffalo hide around his horse's neck. While riding, he would lean forward and rest his elbow in the sling on one side of the horse. He then hooked one foot over the horse's back and could stay on the moving horse this way. Both of his hands were then free to shoot arrows. Sometimes, warriors even surprised their enemies by shooting from between the horse's legs instead of from over its head.

THE LEWIS AND CLARK EXPEDITION

Many of the details we know today about the Great Plains tribes come from notes taken by two famous explorers named Meriwether Lewis and William Clark. From 1804 to 1806, Lewis and Clark traveled from near St. Louis, Missouri, all the way up to North Dakota, and then west to Washington. President Thomas Jefferson sent Lewis and Clark to explore these lands and take notes about the people and places they discovered.

53

The president wanted to expand the young United States of America across the continent and was interested in learning about the natural resources of the land. He especially wanted to know if the Missouri River could be used as a major transportation route to move goods by boat to the Pacific Ocean.

WORDS TO KNOW

species: a group of plants or animals that are closely related and look the same.

Lewis and Clark were on a mission of science and discovery, so they were not threatening to the Native American tribes they encountered. They came in peace and the Native Americans responded by offering help. They helped Lewis and Clark identify different **species** of animals and plants so they could record the proper names in writing.

> They also told them the best routes to travel, making their journey much easier than it otherwise might have been.

SACAGAWEA

One Native American named Sacagawea was especially helpful to the Lewis and Clark expedition. Sacagawea was a Shoshone Indian, born in the Rocky Mountains. At about age 10, she was kidnapped and later sold to a French-Canadian fur trapper named Toussaint Charbonneau. Sacagawea and Charbonneau eventually married. They met Lewis and Clark in the Dakotas.

The explorers asked Sacagawea for help trading with the Native Americans. They knew they would need to do more trading as they headed west through Sacagawea's homeland, so Lewis and Clark asked Sacagawea to join them as an interpreter. She didn't speak English, but she did speak French. Sacagawea spoke in Shoshone or Hidatsa with the many Native American groups they encountered and then translated their words into French, which her husband could translate into English for Lewis and Clark.

DID YOU KNOW?

Lewis and Clark recorded 178 new plant species, including the buffaloberry and western red cedar, and 122 new animals such as the black-billed magpie and the pronghorn antelope.

In addition to interpreting, Sacagawea showed Lewis and Clark trails and shortcuts that she remembered from her childhood and helped them find plants for food and medicine. She was so helpful that she stayed with Lewis and Clark all the way to the Pacific Ocean and back.

Without Sacagawea, the tribes Lewis and Clark encountered might have been unfriendly out of fear. Remember, these native people had never seen white-skinned people. With a Native American woman in the group, Lewis and Clark were immediately seen as peaceful. Sacagawea also had a baby along the way, which probably made everyone even less fearful.

🌸 **The image of Sacagawea carrying her baby boy, "Pomp," appears on the Sacagawea gold dollar coin.**

Many historians believe that Sacagawea died soon after the journey, at the age of 25. Others think that she lived under a different name for many decades, until the ripe old age of 100.

BUILD A
MINIATURE BULLBOAT

Native Americans living in the Great Plains, including the Mandan and Hidatsa tribes of the upper Missouri River area, weren't just hunters. They also fished in the many rivers that wind through the Plains. Some of these rivers, like the Missouri and Knife Rivers, are so big that Native Americans needed boats to cross them. It should be no surprise that bison were used in making these boats, called bullboats.

The round frame of the boat was made of willow branches tied together with buffalo hair. Buffalo hide was stretched over the frame. People sat in the boat and paddled with large sticks or used their hands. To tackle the challenge of steering a saucer-shaped boat, a rudder from a piece of wood attached to a buffalo tail did the trick.

SUPPLIES

- aluminum foil
- small bowl
- Popsicle or craft sticks
- tape

A bullboat only weighed about 30 pounds but it was sturdy and could carry heavy loads of supplies up and down rivers. Made with a fresh buffalo hide dried over a wooden frame, it was waterproof and strong enough to paddle through choppy water, even when laden down with firewood or passengers. The hair of the hide on the outside of the boat helped to keep it from spinning, but adding a rudder enabled the boat to move in a straight line.

1 To build your bullboat's hull, take a piece of aluminum foil and place a bowl in its center. Wrap the foil up the sides of the bowl. Add two or three more layers to make it sturdy, and then remove the bowl. You'll have a hollow, rounded hull in the shape of a Native American bullboat.

2 Now, try to make your boat go in a straight line across a bathtub or sink full of water by blowing on it. You may be able to make it go straight, but the boat will probably spin in circles.

3 To get your boat to travel in a straight line without spinning in circles, you'll need to add a rudder. You can do this by taping a Popsicle stick to one side of your hull. Keep testing your boat and try attaching the Popsicle stick at different angles or at different depths until the boat moves straight through the water.

TRY THIS

Now try making a bullboat with a frame. You can use pipe cleaners, drinking straws, or strips cut from a file folder. Using the bowl again, press two or three layers of foil against the inside to line the bowl with foil. Make three circles from your framing material to fit around the inside of the bowl at the bottom, middle, and top. Tape the circles into place. Then crisscross the strips to line the bowl and tape them into place. To make the boat even more sturdy, cover the frame with another layer of foil. Remove the bullboat from the bowl and smooth the foil at the top. When you add a rudder can your bullboat carry a load of supplies across a body of water?

DID YOU KNOW?
When the Europeans arrived in North America, there were 60 million bison freely roaming the Great Plains. Now there are only about 200,000 of these animals living in protected areas and ranches.

MAKE YOUR OWN
DOG TRAVOIS

You can hook up your own miniature travois and see how Native Americans used their dogs to help them pull heavy loads.

SUPPLIES

- 2 sticks about 8 inches long
- heavy string
- scissors
- cardboard
- hole punch
- small items to carry on your travois

1 Cross the two sticks together to form an X. The sticks should cross closer to one end so there is a long and a short end of the X. Tie the X together in that shape using the string.

2 Cut a piece of cardboard that will fit between the two sticks in the middle of the long end. Punch holes in each of the 4 corners.

3 Secure the cardboard platform to the sticks with string. Make sure to leave enough room at the bottom so the sticks can drag on the ground with the cardboard platform well up off the ground. Tie the small items to the platform.

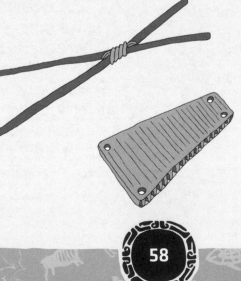

4 Use string to attach the travois to your finger, as shown in the illustration. The smaller side of the X should stick up.

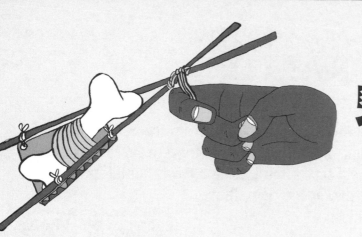

5 Pull the travois along and see if it supports the load. If not, what do you need to change to make it work?

TRY THIS

Using what you learned from making a miniature travois, build a large one that you can use to pull heavy loads. You will need two long sticks or poles about twice as long as you are tall. What material should you use to create a platform? A solid piece of wood will be strong, but heavy. Cloth or netting might work well, or several small sticks tied across the long ends of the travois. Experiment with different ways to create a platform. Then tie on the load you want to move. Now, how can you pull the travois? Can you figure out a way to attach it to your chest or your waist? Now get pulling!

DID YOU KNOW?

There is some evidence that early Native Americans figured out how to create rope-like cords from tree roots. They probably used these cords to tie up bundles of freshly picked herbs, to weave into baskets, to hang animal hides out to dry before turning them into blankets and clothing, and to create fishing lines.

CREATE YOUR OWN
RATTLE

Native American parents made toys for their children from the things they found in nature. One of the more common toys was a rattle made from the hoof and skin of a buffalo. You can make a similar rattle using a cow's hoof. If possible, use a thick piece of cloth. The thicker the cloth, the more it will resemble buffalo hide.

SUPPLIES

- piece of cloth
- scissors
- uncooked rice
- cow's hoof (found in the dog treat section of any local pet store)

1 Cut your piece of cloth into a large square that can be wrapped around the entire cow's hoof. Cut a second piece of cloth into a strip about 2 feet long (60 centimeters).

2 Fill the open side of the cow's hoof halfway with uncooked rice, and then wrap the cloth tightly around it.

3 Use the strip of cloth to tie the bigger piece of cloth as tightly as possible. You want it to be taut across the open side of the hoof, like a drum. Then the rice can bounce off the cloth the same way it bounces off the insides of a buffalo hoof.

4 Practice shaking your rattle in different ways. What kind of rhythms can you make?

TRY THIS

Make another rattle using another grain or dried beans instead of rice. Is the sound different? In what way? What happens if you cover your rattle with a piece of leather or a different kind of cloth? Or use something else from nature in place of a cow's hoof. Use your imagination and have some fun with several different rattles and a group of friends!

CHAPTER 6

The Southwest and Mesoamerican Tribes

THE HOHOKAM, MOGOLLON, ANASAZI, MAYA, AZTEC, PIMA, TOHONO O'ODHAM, HOPI, APACHE & NAVAJO

The tribes living in what is now the southwestern United States and northern Mexico had to adapt to a harsh desert climate. Blazing summer temperatures could reach 120 degrees Fahrenheit during the day (49 degrees Celsius), while cold winter nights dropped down to 25 degrees Fahrenheit (-4 degrees Celsius).

Though the region was very dry, the tribes were able to control the water to grow crops. Some used **irrigation** systems while others became experts at farming in dry conditions. They cultivated squash and beans and 24 different varieties of maize.

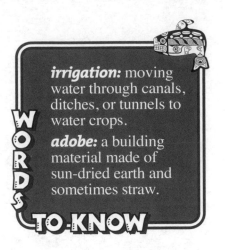

WORDS TO KNOW

irrigation: moving water through canals, ditches, or tunnels to water crops.

adobe: a building material made of sun-dried earth and sometimes straw.

The soil in the area was rich in clay. The Southwest tribes used this natural resource to build **adobe** homes and to make the beautiful pottery they are famous for today.

EARLY SOUTHWEST CULTURES

The Hohokam, Mogollon, and Anasazi cultures of New Mexico, Arizona, Colorado, and Utah represent early civilizations in the southwestern United States and the start of a settled farming life. Each culture was different but all had customs and tools similar to those discovered in nearby Mesoamerica.

The Three Sisters

Why do you think the Native Americans called maize, squash, and beans the Three Sisters? Because they get along well when they are planted together. The bean vines climb up the corn stalks for support, while the squash plants cover the ground below the beans and corn. The large leaves of the squash plants keep out the weeds and shade the soil to keep it from drying out.

The Hohokam dominated the region around the Salt and Gila Rivers in Arizona for 2,000 years. Beginning around 400 BCE, they established villages, built temple mounds, and developed an extensive irrigation system. But by 1450 CE, the Hohokam culture vanished from the area and experts don't know why. The name Hohokam means "vanished ones."

Without metal tools and without horses to help them, the Hohokam built the largest and most advanced irrigation system in the Americas. They learned to capture and control water in the desert by building dams out of muddy, clay earth and floodgates out of woven mats strung

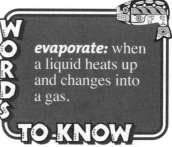

WORDS TO-KNOW

evaporate: when a liquid heats up and changes into a gas.

across the rivers. They dug narrow, deep canals to direct the flow of water instead of wide, shallow ones. This helped prevent water from **evaporating** in the hot desert sun. They lined canals with clay, which hardened to keep water from seeping into the dirt along the sides.

This made their canals a lot like the water pipes we use today.

The Hohokam grew corn, cotton, beans, and squash. Like the Mesoamerican cultures, corn was a **staple** in the Hohokam diet. An important Hohokam tool was the metate and mano, which they used to grind corn. A metate is a stone with a curved, bowl-like shape. A mano is a smooth, handheld stone used to grind grains in the metate.

staple: an important part of a diet.

Early Hohokam families lived in single-room pit houses dug into the ground, framed with saplings, and covered with mud. Family groups of aunts, uncles, cousins, and grandparents arranged their homes around a rectangular courtyard, where they wove baskets and made pottery and stone tools. Later, they built dried mud houses entirely above ground.

>•✦•◄ Like the Maya, Hohokam villages had sunken ball courts where they played team sports using a rubber ball.

For a thousand years beginning about 300 BCE, the Mogollon settled in the mountains, forests, and deserts east of the Hohokam in Arizona, New Mexico, Texas, and northern Mexico. The Mogollon grew the typical crops of corn, beans, and squash, but they often had to rely on other sources of food. High in the mountains, rainfall was plentiful but the growing season was short. Rainfall was unpredictable in the lower mountain river valleys and along the desert river basins, where the growing season was longer.

DID YOU KNOW?

Every Hohokam village had a pit oven called an *horno*. The oven was heated to extremely high temperatures with a wood fire and then covered with dirt to keep in the heat while the food cooked.

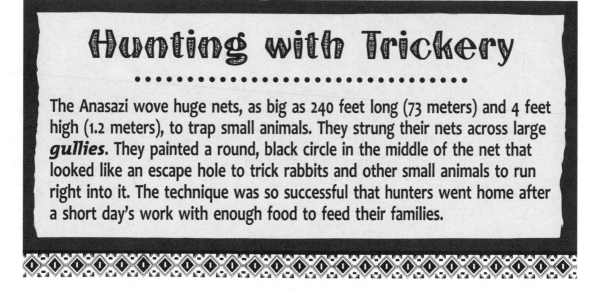

Hunting with Trickery

The Anasazi wove huge nets, as big as 240 feet long (73 meters) and 4 feet high (1.2 meters), to trap small animals. They strung their nets across large *gullies.* They painted a round, black circle in the middle of the net that looked like an escape hole to trick rabbits and other small animals to run right into it. The technique was so successful that hunters went home after a short day's work with enough food to feed their families.

But there was plenty of wild game to hunt, including bighorn sheep, antelope, beaver, turkey, and deer. Edible seeds, nuts, prickly pear fruit, and wild tomatoes were also an important part of the Mogollon diet.

➤◈✠◈◄ Like the Hohokam, early Mogollon lived in single-family pit houses grouped in villages. Later, the Mogollon built large cliff dwellings high up in natural caves with many families living together.

WORDS TO KNOW

gully: a deep, narrow valley between hills or mountains.

pueblo: a communal village consisting of one or more flat-roofed structures of stone or adobe, arranged in terraces and housing a number of families.

The Mogollon were conquered by the Anasazi, the third original Southwest culture. Meaning "ancient people" in the Hopi language, the Anasazi first lived in pit houses as early as 1200 BCE. Later they built huge adobe buildings called *pueblos* the size of modern apartment buildings that housed as many as a thousand people.

Pueblos had holes in their ceilings for entering and exiting and people climbed in and out and from room to room on ladders. People living in these dwellings became known as the Pueblo people.

Pueblo Bonito, or the "Beautiful Village" is one of the most famous Anasazi structures. You can visit Pueblo Bonito's ruins in Chaco Canyon, in the northwest part of New Mexico. You'll also see evidence there of the old pit houses, which the Anasazi later turned into **kivas** where families gathered for work, play, and ceremonies.

WORDS TO KNOW

kiva: a large room partially underground used for religious and other purposes.

✤ Pueblo Bonito had 800 rooms and was home to 1,200 Anasazi. A structure called Cliff Palace in Mesa Verde had 200 rooms where 1,000 Pueblo people lived. These sprawling structures were like houses full of closets, with most of the rooms used for storage. The living space was outside during good weather.

GREAT MESOAMERICAN CITIES

As these early southwestern civilizations were forming into small cities around 200 CE, Native Americans farther south in Mesoamerica were already living in huge cities. Many archaeologists believe that the cities of the Maya and Aztec people in the south inspired the northern tribes to build bigger settlements.

The first great Native American city was the Maya city of Tikal, meaning "Place of Voices" or "Place of Tongues" in Mayan. Tikal spanned 23 square miles (60 square kilometers). Experts believe as many as 200,000 Maya lived in Tikal among its palaces, temples, ball courts, and plazas. **Aqueducts** and **cisterns** provided fresh water to residents the way underground pipes do for city residents today.

Tikal contained about 200 upright stone slabs known as **stelae**. The Maya carved elaborate **hieroglyphs** into the stelae describing the lives and achievements of city rulers.

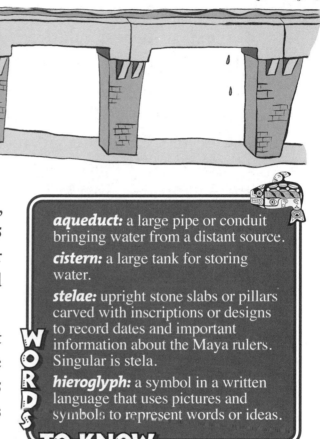

WORDS TO KNOW

aqueduct: a large pipe or conduit bringing water from a distant source.

cistern: a large tank for storing water.

stelae: upright stone slabs or pillars carved with inscriptions or designs to record dates and important information about the Maya rulers. Singular is stela.

hieroglyph: a symbol in a written language that uses pictures and symbols to represent words or ideas.

DID YOU KNOW?

You can visit the Gila Cliff Dwellings National Monument in the Gila Wilderness in Silver City, New Mexico. The homes and surroundings still look very much like they did when the Mogollon lived in the area. Most of the wood in the dwellings is original, dating from trees cut down between 1276 and 1287.

The stelae were impressive, but even more impressive were the city's pyramids. Tikal's pyramids towered up to 230 feet high (70 meters) and were probably the tallest man-made structures ever built by Native Americans. Imagine the backbreaking work of laying massive stone upon stone to build these pyramids without modern-day machinery.

Why did Tikal began to fall into ruin around 900 CE? War, **drought**, or **overpopulation** were all possible causes. Around the same time another of the first great cities, Teotihuacán, was also in decline.

The Aztec city of Teotihuacán was built around 100 CE, about 30 miles northeast of present-day Mexico City (50 kilometers). The Aztec people lived in Teotihuacán, which means City of the Gods, but they didn't build it. Nobody is quite sure who did. What we do know is that Teotihuacán was a powerful force in the region that some historians compare to the **Roman Empire**.

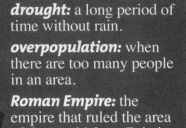

drought: a long period of time without rain.

overpopulation: when there are too many people in an area.

Roman Empire: the empire that ruled the area of the world from Britain and Germany to North Africa and the Persian Gulf, from about 27 BCE to 393 CE.

WORDS TO KNOW

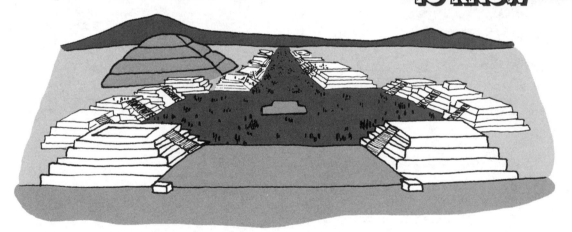

The city spanned about 8 square miles and housed as many as 200,000 residents (13 square kilometers). The Avenue of the Dead was the main street and ran through the city for 2 miles (3 kilometers). City streets and alleys were paved in stone, and the temples were almost as steep as mountain cliffs. The people of Teotihuacán wrote books, counted numbers using bars and dots, observed a 260-day calendar, and enjoyed a chocolate drink.

◈ As in Tikal, the most striking structures in Teotihuacán were the pyramids. The city's Pyramid of the Sun remains the third-largest pyramid in the world.

After the mysterious decline of Teotihuacán sometime before 1000 CE, it was many years before the Aztecs began construction on Tenochtitlán, the third major city of the Americas. Aztec history predicted that its people would find the site for their great city in the place where they encountered an eagle perched on a cactus, devouring a snake. Around 1325 CE, at Lake Texcoco in the Mexican Highlands, the Aztecs came upon that exact scene. They immediately began building Tenochtitlán right in the middle of the lake. The city was eventually home to 200,000 people.

WORDS TO KNOW

causeway: a raised road across water or wet ground.

DID YOU KNOW?

To help feed their large population, the Aztecs used chinampas, or floating gardens. These were built by fencing rectangular areas in the shallow lake with walls made of wattle. The rectangles were filled with mud until they were higher than the water level. Roots of plants growing down from the chinampas anchored them to the lake bottom.

To connect their island to the mainland, the Aztecs built raised **causeways** of sand, dirt, and rocks. They built aqueducts on top of the causeways to bring in freshwater because they couldn't drink the salty water from Lake Texcoco.

Tenochtitlán flourished until 1521, when Spanish explorer Hernán Cortés and his army captured the city and destroyed most of its original buildings.

The God Quetzalcoatl

Quetzalcoatl was as important to the religion of Mesoamerica as Jesus Christ is to Christianity. In most stories Quetzalcoatl is the Feathered Serpent and one of the main gods of all civilization. He is the god of intelligence, the wind, merchants, and arts and crafts. He is also the morning star and a giver of life who created mankind from the bones of failed civilizations. He invented books and the calendar, and he created maize for everyone to eat.

Both the Maya and Aztecs worshipped the Feathered Serpent and waited for him to return. When Hernán Cortés arrived from Spain, the Aztecs believed he was Quetzalcoatl. They treated him as a god instead of an invader and gave him lavish gifts.

MODERN DESCENDANTS

The Pima and Tohono O'Odham tribes were descendants of the Hohokam. They lived near the Gila River in Arizona, but their area of influence extended all the way to Mexico. The two tribes were close friends and expert makers of watertight baskets. The Tohono O'Odham are also known as the Papago, which comes from the word *papah*, meaning "beans," and *ootam*, meaning "people."

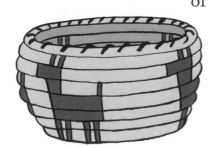

The Pima were peaceful people, but when attacked, they fought back with stone, glass, and iron spear points on their arrows. They also used war clubs and shields made of rawhide.

Pima tradition tells of a massive flood that left only one husband and wife of the tribe living. They had enough children of their own to help the tribe continue. According to the traditions of the tribe, an owl carried the souls of the dead away, and so the Pima feared hooting birds, believing they were signs of death on the way.

Like the Pima, the Tohono O'Odham of southern Arizona were peaceful farmers. They also relied on the desert cactus to survive. Using a long pole made of dried saguaro cactus ribs called a *kuibit*, they knocked the sweet fruit off flowering saguaro cacti. They ate the fruit raw, like candy, or they boiled it to make syrup or jam. Sometimes they dried the fruit and ground it into a powder they mixed with water, sort of like the powdered lemonade mix you find in supermarkets today.

The best-known descendants of the Anasazi culture were the Hopi, a tribe whose name means "Peaceful Ones." The Hopi lived in Arizona, building their pueblos on **mesas** that could be easily defended against enemy tribes. These settlements were similar to the pueblos built by their Anasazi ancestors.

WORDS TO KNOW

mesa: a wide flat area on top of a hill with one or more cliff-like sides.

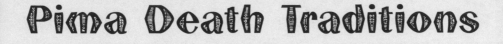

Pima Death Traditions

The Pima followed a special custom when a member of their tribe died. The person was buried in a sitting position, facing east, surrounded by favorite foods and possessions for the journey to the next life. Everything else a person had, including his or her home, was destroyed. Members of the tribe were not permitted to speak the person's name until long after his or her death. The Pima believed that even mentioning this person's name brought back all the sorrow associated with the death. Also, no future children could be named for someone who died.

Like the Anasazi, the Hopi farmed corn, squash, beans, and tobacco. They used a long digging stick called a dibble to plant corn in the desert soil where they lived. Hopi farmers made narrow holes at least a foot deep (30 centimeters), to reach the damp subsoil. After dropping 10 to 20 seeds into the hole, the farmer packed it tightly with dirt. This created a cool, wet environment protected from the desert sun.

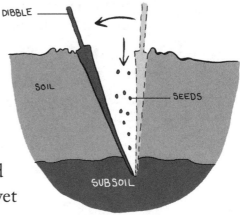

The seeds sprouted deep roots that served as strong anchors after the plants burst through the topsoil where they had to stand up to the desert wind.

Making Piki

• •

The Hopi used corn to cook piki, a paper-thin bread they dipped into stews of squash, beans, wild sagebrush, milkweed, watercress, and dandelions. To make piki batter, the women mixed cornmeal with water and wood ash. The cook heated a slab of sandstone called a *duma* above a fire. When the duma was just the right temperature, the cook spread the batter on it by hand, then quickly lifted it off with her fingers so it wouldn't burn. She then rolled the piki into a cylinder shape before it dried out and cracked into little pieces. Good dumas were prized possessions, passed down for generations, and being able to make proper piki was a highly valued skill.

WARRIORS FROM THE NORTH

The Pima, Tohono O'Odham, Hopi, and other tribes in the southwestern United States lived quite peacefully until the Apache and Navajo tribes migrated to the area from Canada sometime after 1000 CE.

The warriors of the Apache and Navajo tribes raided the pueblos and quickly came to dominate the region. These warriors took everything: cotton blankets, woven baskets, pottery, turquoise beads, farming tools, silver jewelry, sheep, and horses. They were especially aggressive about capturing sheep, which they learned to shear for wool to spin into yarn for cloth and blankets.

The Apaches spread across the southern Plains into Colorado, Arizona, New Mexico, and northern Mexico, while the Navajo people moved into Arizona, New Mexico, and part of Utah.

The Apache were nomadic people who hunted deer and buffalo. They lived in shelters called wickiups, which were dome-shaped and made of wooden poles covered with brush or reed mats. Some Apache covered their wickiups with buffalo hides.

The Apache were known as fierce warriors with a reputation for amazing **endurance**. Some stories say Apache warriors could run 50 miles without stopping (80 kilometers). They fought with neighboring tribes, and then with the Spanish, who tried to kidnap them to work as slaves in the silver mines in Mexico.

WORDS TO KNOW

endurance: the ability to withstand something difficult for a long time.

Geronimo

The most famous Apache warrior was a man called Geronimo. His original name was Goyathlay, or "The One Who Yawns," given to him because of his easygoing nature. He lived a peaceful life until he turned 27, in 1858, when Mexican troops trying to take over Apache lands murdered Goyathlay's entire family. He swore revenge. Goyathlay led raids on Mexican and U.S. settlements until he finally surrendered in 1886. Mexican soldiers mysteriously nicknamed him Geronimo, the Spanish name for Jerome.

After U.S. soldiers took control of Apache lands, leaders of the country sought out Geronimo as a symbol of the Native American heritage that had once existed in the Southwest. President Theodore Roosevelt even brought him to Washington, D.C., in 1905, to participate in the inaugural parade. Souvenir bows, arrows, and pins were sold with Geronimo's image. He died in 1909.

The Navajo called themselves Dineh, or "the people." They lived in hexagonal or **octagonal** houses called hogans built from logs and finished with mud plaster. Every hogan was built with the door facing east so families could wake each morning with the light. If a person died in a hogan, it was usually burned.

W O R D S

TO KNOW

octagonal: eight sided.

famine: a period of great hunger and lack of food for a large population.

The first Navajo were farmers who grew corn, beans, and other crops. Later they also raised and herded sheep. The Navajo often clashed with the Spanish settlers who came in search of gold.

The Navajo people created beautiful sand paintings, often so large and detailed they took 15 men a full day to make. They were created to remove spells believed to cause **famine**, disease, death, and other bad things.

Medicine men sprinkled colored sand within the bounds of a circle. Depending on the spells that needed to be removed, the artists created different pictures on top of this circle with red, white, yellow, black, and blue powders. The powders were made by mixing pollen, cornmeal, ground charcoal, and ground-up minerals.

When the dry painting was complete, any person who needed a spell removed sat on it. A medicine man danced around the person, shaking a rattle, praying, and chanting. When the ceremony was over, the painting—along with the offending spells—was destroyed. Each participant kept a pinch of sand, believing that it contained healing powers.

UNDERSTANDING IRRIGATION

In some parts of the world, such as the desert areas where the Hohokam farmers lived, irrigation systems are needed so that crops receive the water they need. Experiment with different irrigation systems by planting seeds in containers of different shapes and sizes and watching how well the seeds grow. Choose containers made from different materials, such as paper, clay, and plastic.

SUPPLIES

- science journal and pencil
- planting containers of varying shape, size, and material
- bean seeds
- potting mix
- measuring cups
- plastic wrap
- rubber bands
- water

1 Start a scientific method worksheet in your science journal. The scientific method is the way that scientists ask questions and then find answers. If you want to grow a plant with the least amount of water, what size and shape is the best choice for your container? Is there a container material that will retain water better than others? Make your predictions and then start planting.

2 Fill the containers with potting mix and plant a few seeds in each.

3 Water each container with the same amount of water so the soil is evenly damp. Cover the containers with plastic wrap and secure it with a rubber band.

4 Observe your seeds every day and watch for signs that the dirt is getting dry. Water each container with exactly the same amount of water each day.

5 Keep the soil moist and your containers out of direct sunlight until your seeds sprout. Once you have seedlings you can remove the plastic and start to move them into more direct light. You can leave them in direct light more and more each day for about a week until they are used to full sunlight.

Plastic	clay	paper
DAY1 ½ c.	1 c.	¼ c.
DAY2		
DAY3		
DAY4		

6 Record the amount of water you use in each container every day, as well as your observations. Compare how your containers retain water and which of your seeds grows faster. What conclusions can you draw about irrigation techniques?

TRY THIS

Using what you learned, try the experiment again. Are there other ways to water your plants? Try using only containers with holes in the bottom. Place them in dishes of water and let the soil draw up water as needed. Is plant growth affected by the size and shape of the dish of water?

CREATE YOUR OWN
HIEROGLYPHICS

Hieroglyphics are line drawings of pictures or symbols that represent words, syllables, or ideas. The Maya carved them into slabs of rock to tell stories and record their history.

Hieroglyphics can be difficult to understand, especially if you do not know the history and beliefs of the people who created them. What does a picture of an eagle represent? That someone flew somewhere or saw a soaring bird in the sky? Or maybe the people who created the hieroglyphics believed the eagle represented bravery and used it to show that a person fought well during battle. Understanding a culture is often essential to understanding their hieroglyphics.

Tell your own stories with your own hieroglyphics. You might describe your morning with pictures that represent getting out of bed, eating breakfast, and brushing your teeth. What hieroglyphics might work for those scenes? Be creative! Your hieroglyphics don't have to be perfect representations. They can be your own interpretation of an aspect of your life.

SUPPLIES

• pen or pencil
• scrap paper
• construction paper

WAKE UP IN
THE MORNING

GET OUT
OF BED

1 Think about what you want to write a story about, then create the hieroglyphics that you can use to tell the story.

2 Using these hieroglyphic symbols of your own, write the story—either an account of something that happened to you today, something you hope for in the future, a memorable event in your life, or a game you played in the past. See how many hieroglyphic symbols you can reuse from line to line within your story.

3 Try to keep your language as simple as possible, and then show your creations to friends and see if they understand what you've written.

TRY THIS

Do the project with friends and then combine all the glyphs created by the group. Now create new stories using your larger collection of symbols.

EAT BREAKFAST

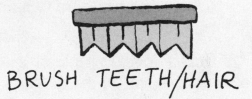

BRUSH TEETH/HAIR

DID YOU KNOW?

The Maya city of Tikal is considered an archaeological wonder of the world. It is often grouped with Machu Picchu in Peru, Petra in Jordan, and the Great Wall of China.

CREATE YOUR OWN
NAVAJO JEWELRY

The Navajo are well known for their art, especially sand painting, weaving, and jewelry making. In this activity you will make beads that represent the sacred colors of the Navajo compass. North is black, south is turquoise, east is white, and west is yellow.

1 Cut four triangles measuring 1 inch (2½ centimeters) at the base by approximately 3 inches high (7½ inches) out of each color of construction paper. You'll have 12 triangles.

2 Take a toothpick and roll each triangle around the toothpick very tightly, starting at the base. Put a dot of white glue at the point of the rolled up paper and hold it for several seconds. Take out the toothpick. You should have a tube-shaped bead.

3 Paint a clear coat of nail polish on each bead. While the beads are drying cut a piece of string about 2 feet long (60 centimeters). Attach a piece of masking tape at the end so the beads won't fall off the end of the string.

4 When all the beads are dry, thread them onto the string in a pattern. Remove the masking tape and tie the ends of the string together. Make sure the string is long enough to go over your head before you tie it!

CHAPTER 7

The Pacific Northwest Tribes
THE NUU-CHAH-NULTH, MAKAH & TLINGIT

The Pacific Northwest is one of the most beautiful regions of North America. Sprawling forests of deep-green fir trees blanket the mountains, and snow-capped peaks reach beyond the clouds into the heavens. Just offshore are chains of islands and protected harbors, and all along the coast is a network of trails where hikers can photograph black bears and bald eagles.

It's no surprise that the word *rugged* is often used to describe this part of the continent. The terrain is dense with forests, mountains, and rock formations that make farming difficult or even impossible. Because of these conditions, the Native Americans that settled in this area focused on hunting, gathering, and fishing to survive.

※ Eventually, as the tribes came into contact with each another, they also used trade as a tool of survival.

GONE FISHING

There were more than two dozen tribes in the Pacific Northwest, including the Haida, Makah, Nuu-chah-nulth, Tsimshian, Tlingit, Tillamook, Chinook, Älsé, Coos, and Coquille. They had one important thing in common—fishing. Every spring, the salmon *spawn* in this part of North America. There was a time when hundreds of thousands of salmon made their way back from the ocean to the rivers where they were born to lay eggs. They swam together in schools through the region's waterways.

WORDS TO KNOW

spawn: to produce and deposit eggs.

DID YOU KNOW?

Because of hydroelectric dams in Washington's Olympic Peninsula, spawning habitats for Pacific salmon disappeared. The salmon population fell from 400,000 to just 3,000. But the United States has begun removing the dams and salmon are returning to the area. Sacred lands of the Lower Elwha Klahlam tribe, which were flooded when the dams were built, have been returned to the tribe.

LONGHOUSES

Wood was plentiful from the area's forests, and longhouses built from cedar planks were a common form of housing for many tribes of the Pacific Northwest. Each clan had its own longhouse, which was sometimes as long as 100 feet or more (30 meters). Clans often decorated the outside of their longhouse with beautiful clan symbols. Inside the longhouse, private spaces for each family were created with hanging mats made from cedar bark. In some Pacific Northwest tribes, the tribe built the longhouse and the chief or head of the tribe assigned space in the longhouse to individual families. In others, individual members of the tribe built their own longhouses and assigned their own family members space within the longhouse.

Rivers were so clogged with fish that a person could not enter the water without stepping on one. Bears sat on the riverbanks and simply scooped their paws into the water and picked up salmon to eat, like you or I might do at a cafeteria buffet.

The fact that the salmon spawn every year at the same time made fishing in this region reliable. All of the Native American tribes that lived here developed tools to catch as many fish as possible and to preserve their catch to eat throughout the cold winters when it was hard to find food.

HOW SALMON SPAWN

Salmon are anadromous, which means they return from the ocean where they live to the rivers where they were born in order to **breed**. Salmon swim for years and for thousands of miles in the ocean, but they always find their way back to their birthplace. Some experts believe salmon navigate by way of smell, while others believe they are especially sensitive to the earth's magnetic field and their brains work like a compass. Nobody knows for sure.

As salmon swim from salt water back into freshwater, their appearance changes. The males develop a curved mouth with large canine teeth, and the females and males both change color, from silver to black. Some males develop a hump on their back.

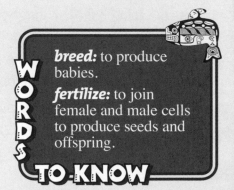

WORDS TO KNOW

breed: to produce babies.

fertilize: to join female and male cells to produce seeds and offspring.

The males and females form pairs as they make their way upriver. The male's job is to protect the female while the female creates a nest in the gravel riverbed by sweeping her tail back and forth across it. This spawning area, which can be 10 feet long (3 meters) and 6 feet wide (almost 2 meters), is called a redd.

Once the redd is complete, the female releases her eggs at the same time the male releases his milt, or sperm. The eggs are **fertilized** in the water as they float down into the redd. The female then sweeps the area with her tail again to cover and protect the fertilized eggs with gravel. The parent salmon die soon after spawning. The eggs hatch within one to three months, and the cycle of life begins anew.

FISHING TECHNIQUES

Do you like to fish? In the fishing tribes of the Pacific Northwest, it was up to the men to catch the fish and the women to preserve them. The simplest way for a man to catch a fish is with his bare hands, just as the black bears do with their claws. But the men wanted to catch more than one fish at a time, so they invented tools to help them.

A dip net is one of the most basic fishing tools. A bag of netting is attached to a Y- or V-shaped frame made from branches. Then the fish can be scooped out of the river.

To catch more fish with less effort, Native Americans invented the **weir**. This wooden trap could be laid across the entire width of a stream or river. It had holes large enough to let the river's water flow through but too small to allow fish to escape. The flow of the river pushed the fish into the weir, where fishermen waited to collect them. Some fish got through, but many of them were caught.

Native Americans of the Pacific Northwest speared the fish caught in their weirs with a **leister**. This spear has three prongs arranged like the points of a triangle. With three sharp tips instead of one, it was much easier to spear a wriggling fish on the first try. To make it easier to see and spear fish caught in a weir in murky water, fishermen lay slabs of white quartz on the river bottom to create a bright backdrop.

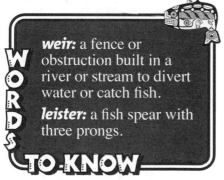

WORDS TO-KNOW

weir: a fence or obstruction built in a river or stream to divert water or catch fish.

leister: a fish spear with three prongs.

Weirs in the East

Weirs were not only used in the Pacific Northwest. In what is today the city of Boston, Massachusetts, scientists have found evidence of a huge weir used by Native Americans. The remnants of this weir show that those who made it found or cut sticks of wood 4–6 feet long (1.2–1.8 meters), then whittled them sharp on one end and stuck them a few feet apart (1 meter) into the clay bed beneath the water. Judging by its size, scientists estimate that it contained 65,000 sticks.

PRESERVING THE CATCH

Of course, some fish was cooked and eaten immediately. But the rest had to be preserved. How did the Native Americans make their fish last throughout the winter? The women were experts at saving every last morsel and their methods were brilliant.

To boil the great quantity of fish caught in spawning season, women lined up canoes that had been carved out of tree trunks. They filled the canoes with water and fish. Using long wooden tongs, they placed rocks that had been heated in a fire into the canoes until the water boiled.

As the fish boiled, their oil rose to the top of the water. Using wooden ladles, the women skimmed the oil off the top and stored it in watertight wooden boxes. This oil was used to cook and season food, make medicines, or trade with other tribes.

After boiling, the women used a blade made of bone to remove the head, tail, fins, and guts of each fish. Then the fish were hung outside on wooden drying frames. After drying in the sun, the fish were smoked over a fire. This long process preserved the fish so the meat wouldn't spoil.

OTHER FOOD SOURCES

The Native Americans of the Pacific Northwest didn't eat only salmon. Two tribes in particular, the Nuu-chah-nulth (also known as the Nootka) and the Makah, were known as great whale hunters.

The Nuu-chah-nulth and Makah lived on Vancouver Island and throughout the Olympic Peninsula. They built long, strong wooden canoes for their whale hunts. Because whale meat and **blubber** were so important to these tribes, whale hunters were highly regarded. The position of **harpooner** was extremely important and the honor was **inherited** from one's father.

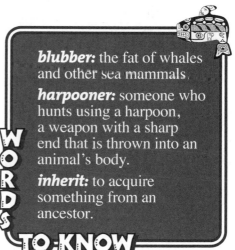

WORDS TO KNOW

blubber: the fat of whales and other sea mammals.

harpooner: someone who hunts using a harpoon, a weapon with a sharp end that is thrown into an animal's body.

inherit: to acquire something from an ancestor.

During the hunt, each harpooner carried an 18-foot-long wooden harpoon (5½ meters). A blade of mussel shells and bone spurs jutted out from the tip. Lengths of rope attached to the other end of the harpoon were connected to large floats, like balloons, made of sealskin.

Whale hunting was a difficult, dangerous job. The hunters paddled out to a whale—which was no small feat—and positioned their canoes so the harpooner had a clear shot. Several canoes attacked the same whale at once to increase the chance of a successful hunt. With the harpooners in position, they tried to spear the whale. On a lucky day, more than one harpoon stuck into the great mammal.

The wounded whale would dive beneath the surface, taking the harpoons with it. The hunters then threw the sealskin floats that were connected to the harpoons overboard. The floats made it harder for the whale to swim below the surface and prevented the whale from sinking after it died.

> Once the giant animal stopped breathing, the hunters paddled back to shore, towing their catch behind them.

It was a joyous occasion filled with songs and drumming as the Nuu-chah-nulth and Makah hunters towed a whale to the beach. Every part of the whale was used. People ate the meat and skin. The **sinew** was braided into rope. The intestines were used as containers to preserve food and the blubber made oil for candles.

WORDS TO KNOW

sinew: a strong band of animal tissue that connects muscles to bones.

TRIBAL TRADE

Because so much food was harvested during one season in the Pacific Northwest, there was time to focus on building **wealth** and preserving tribal history for future generations.

One way for tribes to build wealth was by trading with other tribes. Trade was an enormous part of society for many tribes. The Tlingit not only traded their own goods, but also acted as middlemen for surrounding tribes. When you go to the store to buy something, the store is the middleman. It buys things and then sells them for a higher price.

WORDS TO KNOW

wealth: a large amount of money or great numnber of possessions.

In return for their efforts, the Tlingit traders kept some of the goods for themselves as a type of payment. Some of the trading trips the Tlingit made took many days. They often had to make dangerous river crossings and climb over tall mountains carrying packs on their backs that weighed up to 100 pounds (45 kilograms). Trips were made during winter in terrible weather, when they had to wear snowshoes and keep a sharp lookout for wild animals! There's no question they earned what they kept.

✴ Some trade between Pacific Northwest tribes moved over waterways. Dugout canoes loaded with goods were paddled up and down the coast.

Those who became rich showed off what they had by holding a **potlatch** dinner. During these occasions the host family gave away as many possessions as possible—not out of kindness but to show how much they had. It was believed that the more a person gave away, the more highly he or she would be thought of in society. The richest people in the Tlingit tribes were given a special name, *ankawoo*, meaning "great wealthy person."

WORDS TO KNOW

potlatch: a ceremony, sometimes lasting for several days, at which a host lavishes gifts upon the guests.

toll: a charge to use a passageway, such as a river, road, or bridge.

Potlatches were grand ceremonies that lasted several days. Hundreds of guests attended, some traveling long distances to get there. The hosts would have prepared for several years in advance, gathering gifts to present to each guest. According to legend, at one potlatch a host gave away about 10,000 blankets. Imagine the effort behind so many blankets, when every single one had to be handmade and transported by boat or by foot!

DID YOU KNOW?

Just as the Tlingit acted as middlemen for trade that required travel over land, the Chinook tribe controlled the flow of trade on rivers. It is believed that they charged **tolls** from tribes that canoed past their settlements.

TOTEM POLES

It was important to the Tlingit and other tribes of the Pacific Northwest, such as the Haida and the Tsimshian, to pass down their family and tribal histories through generations. Like the stone stelae found in Mesoamerica that were carved with hieroglyphics, Native American **totem poles** made out of cedar trees were carved with **totems**. These pictures and symbols told a story.

WORDS TO KNOW

totem pole: a pole or post carved and painted with totems.

totem: a carved or painted picture or symbol, often representing a family or clan with a reminder of its history.

Carving a totem pole was an important art passed down through generations.

Totem poles were often put up outside the entrance to a family's dwelling so that everyone would know their history. When a family held a potlatch, for instance, its totem pole helped the guests understand how the family had gained its wealth. The figures on the pole ranged from human faces to animals, each representing something different. While eagles and ravens often represented different clans or families, crows were a symbol of intelligence. Mortuary totem poles honored the dead, and storytelling poles were carved for weddings.

CREATE YOUR OWN
X-RAY ART

In Oregon, the Washo and Wishram tribes passed the time between fishing and hunting by drawing, painting, and carving. The artists in these tribes drew or carved more than just the outline of, say, a fish. They filled that outline with everything they believed to be inside the fish—the bones, organs, and spirits—so that their finished artwork looked like something you might see in a modern x-ray machine. Have an adult supervise while you are on the Internet.

1 Choose an animal that was plentiful in the Pacific Northwest during the time the Washo and Wishram tribes lived there, such as the salmon, black bear, and the bald eagle.

2 Use the Internet to research your chosen animal so that you can represent its insides properly. If you search using the images function in your search engine for bear anatomy or salmon anatomy, plenty of images will come up for you to examine.

3 Be creative and use your imagination. You are creating an abstract work of art that does not have to be perfect and exact!

CREATE YOUR OWN
FAMILY TOTEM POLE

Totem poles convey a family's history. While you can't carve an entire tree as tall as the flagpole outside your school to create a totem pole, you can use the idea of a totem pole to tell your family history.

1 Ask your parents about your family tree. You want to know the names and stories of as many people as possible, including your parents, grandparents, great-grandparents, aunts, and uncles, and anyone else in your family you can learn about.

2 On construction paper, draw or cut out faces or animals representing each person's accomplishments. If you had a particularly brave relative, you might draw a picture of an eagle. For a very funny relative, you might incorporate the face of a clown. After you have created an image for each person in your family history, staple or tape the images together, one above the other, as if on a ladder.

3 Tape your totem pole to the wall so that it climbs as high as possible. If you want to be like the Tlingit of the Pacific Northwest, you can tape it to the wall outside the doorway to your room, so that everyone who walks by or enters will be able to see your family history.

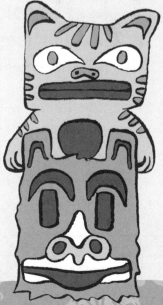

TRY THIS

Create a totem pole to record the story of a family trip, your sports season, a fun day, or other special event.

93

CHAPTER 8

The Arctic Tribes
THE INUIT

hat is the coldest weather you've ever felt? Was it so cold the tip of your nose hurt? Did your fingers or toes turn white and go numb? Think of how thankful you were to get back inside a warm building.

Imagine living where the winter temperature falls to -70 degrees Fahrenheit (-57 Celsius) and the ocean sometimes freezes up to 7 feet deep (2 meters). The wind can be so cold that it freezes human skin on contact. There are no trees, and the only plants are those that grow close to the ground.

For much of the year there is only solid ice and snow as far as the eye can see, so there is no possibility of farming for **sustenance**.

This place, known as the **Arctic**, is at the far northern edge of North America. Scientists believe people have lived within the **Arctic Circle** since around 3000 BCE. Like every other Native American group across the continent, they found creative ways to adapt and survive.

One well-known Arctic tribe is the Inuit, which means "the people." In the face of extreme challenges, the Inuit created a **sustainable** culture in their frigid climate. Why did the Inuit and other Arctic tribes stay in a land of such hardship? Some experts believe that **hostile** tribes to the south prevented them from migrating to a warmer climate. Others think they adapted so well to their environment that they did not need to move.

WORDS TO KNOW

sustenance: something, especially food, that supports life or health.

Arctic: the region around the North Pole within the Arctic Circle.

Arctic Circle: the Arctic Ocean and the surrounding land north of 66 degrees **latitude** north.

latitude: imaginary lines around the earth that measure a position on the earth north or south of the equator.

sustainable: living in a way that has minimal long-term impact on the environment.

hostile: very unfriendly, relating to an enemy.

Eskimo: an insulting nickname given to the northernmost Native Americans by the Algonquian tribes from the south.

DID YOU KNOW?

You may know the Native Americans of the north as **Eskimos**, a name given to them by Algonquians farther south. It's a word that means "eaters of raw meat," and a name that many people of the far north consider insulting. These northern groups, such as the Inuit, prefer to use their tribal names.

The Midnight Sun and Polar Night

Do you live in a place where summer days are longer than winter days? In both **Antarctica** and the Arctic, summer days and winter nights last 24 hours! Maybe you've heard the Arctic called the land of the midnight sun. That's because even at midnight you can see the sun for part of the year. Right around the Arctic Circle, there is one day each summer when the sun does not set at all. The farther north you go, the more days the sun stays above the **horizon**, until you reach the North Pole, where the sun is visible for half the year.

The polar night is the opposite. At the Arctic Circle there is one day each winter when the sun does not rise. The farther north you go, the more days the sun stays below the horizon, until you reach the North Pole where the sun does not rise for half the year. Can you see why there is only one sunrise and one sunset in an entire year at the North Pole?

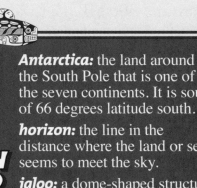

WORDS TO KNOW

Antarctica: the land around the South Pole that is one of the seven continents. It is south of 66 degrees latitude south.

horizon: the line in the distance where the land or sea seems to meet the sky.

igloo: a dome-shaped structure built of blocks of packed snow.

sod: a section of earth with growing grass and roots.

ICE HOUSES

What do you know about Inuit life? Do you think of **igloos**? You might be surprised to learn that these dome-shaped houses were just temporary structures. Most Inuit lived in permanent shelters made of **sod**.

Using **driftwood** or whalebones for frames, the walls of these homes were built with layers of sod collected during the summer when the top layer of earth thawed. Each sod dwelling was built partially underground, giving it a natural form of insulation. Dwellings in a village were grouped together around a **kashim**, used only by the men of the tribe for performing rituals and ceremonies.

Igloos were winter homes used during seal-hunting season. As many as 50 to 60 people, including about 15 hunters, left their sod dwellings for the Arctic Ocean, where the seals lived. The elderly and the sick, and anyone who wasn't physically capable of making the long, difficult journey, stayed behind. There were no trees and no sod in seal country to use to build a shelter, so the Inuits used the only materials available—ice and snow.

DID YOU KNOW?

The Inuit could not depend on plants for food so they hunted year-round. In summer, the Inuit fished from **kayaks** for Arctic char, whitefish, and trout. In the fall, the **caribou** gathered in large herds to migrate, making them easy targets for hunters. Winters meant seal hunting and ice fishing. The Inuit also hunted other animals, including whales, polar bears, and walruses.

Making an Igloo

To make an igloo, the Inuit cleared freshly fallen, loose snow from an area with shovels made of sealskin-covered caribou antlers. This clearing made a "yard" for the igloo with space outside for walking and doing chores. After clearing the patch, workers drew a circle to mark the outline of the igloo's floor.

Next, someone stood inside the circle and began carving into the hard-packed snow with a knife. The goal was to loosen rectangular blocks of hard snow, each about 2 feet long (61 centimeters), 2 feet wide, and 6 inches thick (2½ centimeters). Layers of blocks went around the circle. With each new layer, the blocks were placed a couple of inches closer to the center of the circle until they eventually met overhead to close the roof.

While the walls were being laid from inside the igloo, workers outside the circle packed loose snow into the cracks and holes left between the snow bricks. The soft snow filled the gaps and held the bricks in place. A small hole left in the roof for air to come in also let candle and fire smoke escape. Sometimes a window was made with a clear, freshwater ice block, which the Inuit carried with them from their sod dwellings.

The next task was to dig an entranceway, which always faced south so the fierce north wind didn't blow inside. It only took the Inuit about an hour to build an igloo.

DID YOU KNOW?
The Inuit are known for their beautiful carvings of animals and people. They carve sculptures out of soapstone and other kinds of stone, as well as ivory, bone, and caribou antlers.

Once the igloo was built, the women arranged the inside. A wide mound of packed snow rising 2 or 3 feet above the floor (about 60 to 90 centimeters) provided a sleeping platform. Caribou ribs or waterproof sealskin on top of the mound made a protective dry layer, so the snow didn't melt from the body heat of the sleeping family. Layers of caribou skins went on top of the ribs or sealskin. The bottom layer of skins was laid with the hair facing downward, and the top layer of skins was laid with the hair facing upward, for extra cushioning. Finer skins were used as mats for sitting and on the multi-purpose dining table made of snow blocks.

☆✦ **Large lamps called *qulliq* burned whale blubber to provide light and heat inside an igloo.**

The lamp gave off a flame with almost no smoke. The heat warmed the inside just enough for a thin layer of the wall to melt slightly. It froze into a thin layer of ice, which helped make the igloo stronger. The women used caribou antlers to hang a carved stone pot above the flame to defrost frozen chunks of meat.

While the igloo was warming up and food was being prepared, the women set up racks made of caribou antlers and skin. They used the racks to dry clothes that were wet from snow and ice. To store and dry their ladles and sealskin containers, they pushed sticks into the igloo's walls to make hooks.

SEAL HUNTING

As the women set up camp inside their igloos, the men headed out to hunt for seals. A seal can swim beneath the Arctic ice for 15 to 20 minutes before it needs to find an air hole in the ice to come up to breathe. The Inuit sat at these air holes waiting for seals.

◆ All Inuit hunters had dogs. Their dogs sniffed out the seals' breathing holes.

A hunter widened an air hole with an ice pick made of bear bone. Then he stuck a long, thin caribou antler down to the bottom of the hole to find the area with the thinnest ice. A seal would be more likely to approach where the ice was thin, rather than where there was a thick wall of ice.

DID YOU KNOW?

Boys as young as 10 joined seal-hunting parties, but only the men used weapons.

Once the hunter felt he knew the angle from which the seal would approach, he covered the hole with a layer of fresh snow. He placed a piece of frozen caribou sinew over the hole with a white feather attached. When the feather moved, it meant a seal was trying to get its nose up and into the air hole. Some hunters scratched the ice near the seal's hole to trick a seal swimming underneath the ice into thinking that one of its seal friends was on top of the ice. It could take hours of waiting in subzero Arctic temperatures for the feather to move.

When a seal finally came up through the hole to breathe, the hunter lunged toward the hole with his harpoon. Usually, it took just one try for these hunters to kill a seal that weighed anywhere from 200 to 600 pounds (90 to 270 kilograms). This amount of meat fed a hunter's family for weeks and could be frozen to take with them to the next seal-hunting spot.

DID YOU KNOW?

When a dog found an area of fresh snow that had a breathing hole beneath it, the hunters thrust their harpoons into the snow. The hunter whose harpoon came closest to the hole won the right to hunt it.

SLED DOGS

Eskimo dogs, sometimes called Inuit Huskies, are strong dogs. They have muscular legs, thick necks, and wide chests. Their fur can be any combination of white, black, reddish-brown, and gray. It is double thick compared with other dogs' coats, even on their paws. They needed all that extra fur to stay warm in the climate where they lived and worked.

Males weigh as much as 85 pounds (39 kilograms). They can pull loaded sleds twice their weight 70 miles a day through the snow and ice (120 kilometers). The dogs are also smart and easy to train, which made them good companions for hunters.

Today's descendants of the Eskimo dogs are called Canadian Eskimo dogs. Only a few hundred are believed to be in existence. Modern-day Canadians are so proud of the smart, obedient dogs that they put their picture on a stamp and a 50-cent coin. In some places the dogs still pull sleds.

PLAY A GAME OF
NUGLUKTAQ

Whether the Inuits were at their temporary hunting quarters or at home in their sod dwellings, they enjoyed relaxing after a hard day's work. You can play one of their favorite games, called Nugluktaq.

SUPPLIES

- spool of thread
- group of friends
- skewers

1 Have an adult hold a spool of thread high in the air. Ask the adult to drop the spool while holding on to the end of the thread. The spool will spin as the thread unravels.

2 The players should be waiting beneath the spool, holding the skewers in their hands. The goal of Nugluktaq is to be the first person to stick his or her toothpick or skewer into the hole in the spinning spool. Be careful not to poke each other or the adult holding the string!

You can keep score in single points or in batches, such as the best of three attempts, best of five attempts, and so on.

CHAPTER 9

New Immigrants, Manifest Destiny, and the Trail of Tears

I t can be difficult and sad to learn what happened to many Native Americans and their unique cultures. Over thousands of years, tribes all over the continent had developed complex societies and ways of life.

They invented tools for hunting, farming, fishing, cooking, and carrying food and other supplies. They used the resources around them in ingenious ways to build shelters, make clothing, and create beautiful works of art.

Native American people created languages and used pictures, symbols, and carvings to tell their stories. They developed a rich spiritual life filled with ceremonies, rituals, and stories. They valued the animals that shared their land, and they valued the land itself.

Most Europeans who left their homes to come to the Americas wanted to make a better life for themselves and their families. The truth is, their arrival in North America was the beginning of the end of traditional Native American ways of life.

> As settlers spread across the continent, Native Americans throughout the United States were displaced from their land and from their nature-based culture.

THE SETTLERS MOVE IN

Can you name an early European explorer who landed in North America? What about Christopher Columbus? Columbus sailed from Spain in 1492, with the ships the *Niña*, the *Pinta*, and the *Santa Maria*, on an expedition to find a shorter trade route to the East Indies. When he landed in North America and found people living there, he called them Indios in Spanish, meaning "Indians," thinking he was near India. Columbus was one of many European explorers who traveled the world's oceans from the late 1400s to the early 1800s, looking for new trade routes, new places to build settlements, and new territories to control.

DID YOU KNOW?

The first place Columbus actually landed was on an island in the Caribbean Sea. He then went on to explore Cuba and Hispaniola (now Haiti and the Dominican Republic).

The most famous ship to reach American shores was the *Mayflower*. It landed in Plymouth, Massachusetts, in 1620, carrying **pilgrims** from England seeking a new home where they could freely practice their religion. The Pilgrims encountered the region's Native Americans, called the **Wampanoag**, which means "eastern people."

Their meeting was peaceful and the Wampanoag people helped the Pilgrims. Tradition tells us that these Native Americans enjoyed the first **Thanksgiving** with the Pilgrims in October 1621, following the Pilgrims' first harvest in their new home.

> ❀❖ But the peaceful **coexistence** between the Pilgrims and the Native Americans did not last.

More and more **colonists** arrived and spread across the land, taking it for their own. The Native Americans started to distrust the colonists. By 1675, the relationship between the groups weakened to the point of war, but the Native Americans could not defend themselves against the powerful guns of the colonists. The fighting was just the beginning of what was to come.

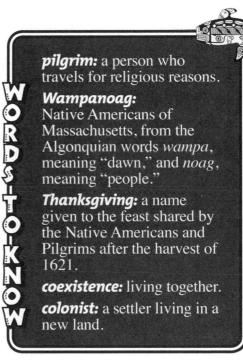

WORDS TO KNOW

pilgrim: a person who travels for religious reasons.

Wampanoag: Native Americans of Massachusetts, from the Algonquian words *wampa*, meaning "dawn," and *noag*, meaning "people."

Thanksgiving: a name given to the feast shared by the Native Americans and Pilgrims after the harvest of 1621.

coexistence: living together.

colonist: a settler living in a new land.

The First Thanksgiving

The feast shared by the Pilgrims and Native Americans in 1621 was a celebration of a successful harvest and a week of hunting. It lasted three days and included turkey, deer, geese, ducks, and swans. Although it was not repeated the following year, it continues to serve as the historical basis for the holiday celebrated in the United States every year on the fourth Thursday of November.

A NEW NATION

The birth of the new United States came 100 years later on July 4, 1776, when the 13 **British colonies** on the East Coast of the United States declared their independence from England. How did people in the colonies begin the process of creating their own nation? They fought the British in the Revolutionary War and eventually won their freedom. As floods of **immigrants** came from Europe to this new country, more and more people pushed westward, creating new settlements on Native American lands.

British colonies: the early English settlements in America.

immigrant: a person who moves to a new country to settle there permanently.

WORDS TO KNOW

All across the continent, Native Americans saw their way of life changing. They started killing large numbers of animals for money and goods rather than hunting just for survival. They traded animal hides to the settlers for food, clothing, alcohol, guns, and jewelry, and soon they were wanting more and more of these items.

The herds of wild animals shrunk as Europeans and Native Americans killed large numbers of them for fur. Native American tribes started fighting among themselves as they struggled to find enough animals to keep up with the demand for fur.

Eventually, the Native Americans realized their way of life was going to become extinct if they continued fighting each other.

Several Native American leaders started talking about **rebellion** against the settlers. Meanwhile, the settlers were calling the Native Americans savages who needed to be controlled.

DID YOU KNOW?

The 13 colonies included Virginia, Massachusetts, New Hampshire, Maryland, Connecticut, Rhode Island, Delaware, North Carolina, South Carolina, New Jersey, New York, Pennsylvania, and Georgia. The land that is now Maine was part of Massachusetts, and the land that is now Vermont was part of New York.

Many people believed that the United States was meant to spread its way of life across North America to the Pacific Ocean and become a huge civilization. This belief was called Manifest Destiny. To gain more land, the United States government began removing the Native Americans from their homelands.

WORDS TO KNOW

rebellion: an act of open or violent resistance.

THE INDIAN REMOVAL ACT

By 1829, when Andrew Jackson became president of the United States, the nation was focused on what it called the Indian Problem. American settlers wanted the Native Americans' land for themselves, while the Native Americans just wanted to hold on to what land they still had.

President Jackson decided to sign the 1830 Indian Removal Act. This law stated that all Native Americans living east of the Mississippi River had to move west, to live on **reservations** in what is now Oklahoma.

Native American tribes, including the Choctaw, Chickasaw, Seminole, Creek, and Cherokee, tried to argue that they were independent people who could not be forced to leave their homelands. In the end they lost their fight and their land.

WORDS TO KNOW

reservation: public land set aside for a special use, such as for the relocation of Native Americans in the 1800s.

THE TRAIL OF TEARS

In 1838, under the direction of President Martin Van Buren, United States troops forced 15,000 Cherokee men, women, and children to march 1,000 miles from Florida and Georgia all the way to Oklahoma (1,600 kilometers). The journey began in October and lasted all winter, until March. Along the way, 4,000 people died.

The Cherokee named this journey the Trail of Tears.

A similar tragedy started farther west, in 1848, when gold was discovered in California. The promise of riches led thousands to settle in the West and the Southwest. The Native Americans living there fought to protect their homeland, but the U.S. army destroyed their fields and their animals. In 1864, about 10,000 Navajo survivors were forced to walk nearly 200 miles to Fort Sumner, in eastern New Mexico (320 kilometers). Many Navajo men, women, and children died.

The only tribe that was at all successful in refusing to leave their homeland was the Seminole. Many Seminole retreated to the swamps of Florida where they fought against U.S. troops between 1835 and 1842. The Seminole killed more than 1,500 American soldiers before the government got tired of fighting over what they considered worthless swampland. Some Seminoles ended up on reservations in the West, but many managed to stay in their homes, where their descendants still live today.

Where the Buffalo Once Roamed

In the Great Plains region, settlers almost completely destroyed the buffalo population. In 1800, when European settlers first began hunting buffalo, it is estimated that there were about 60 million buffalo. By 1870, there were only 13 million buffalo left. In the winter of 1872–1873 more than 1.5 million buffalo hides were shipped east on trains and wagons. By 1900, there were fewer than 1,000 buffalo left. This decline in the buffalo population was *devastating* to the Native Americans of the Great Plains region because they relied on the buffalo for food, tools, shelter, and clothing.

TREATIES AND THE BATTLE OF LITTLE BIGHORN

At first, the United States tried to convince Native Americans to hand over their homelands peacefully. From 1843 to 1852, Governor Isaac Stevenson of the Washington Territory in the Pacific Northwest **negotiated** 52 **treaties** with Native American tribes. These treaties gave the United States the legal right to 157 million acres of land in Idaho, Oregon, and Washington (64 million hectares). Other United States leaders were negotiating similar treaties all across the continent. It wasn't long before the United States came to control nearly every acre of Native American land.

devastating: highly destructive or damaging.

negotiate: to reach agreement by discussion.

treaty: a formal agreement between two parties relating to peace, trade, and/or property.

WORDS TO KNOW

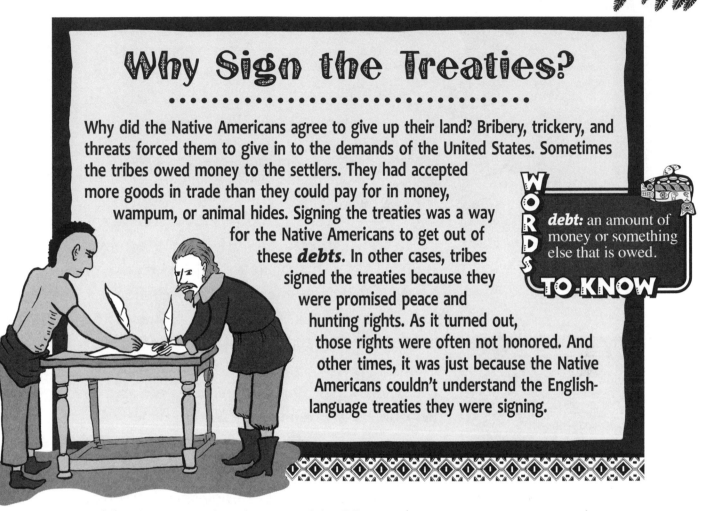

Why Sign the Treaties?

Why did the Native Americans agree to give up their land? Bribery, trickery, and threats forced them to give in to the demands of the United States. Sometimes the tribes owed money to the settlers. They had accepted more goods in trade than they could pay for in money, wampum, or animal hides. Signing the treaties was a way for the Native Americans to get out of these *debts*. In other cases, tribes signed the treaties because they were promised peace and hunting rights. As it turned out, those rights were often not honored. And other times, it was just because the Native Americans couldn't understand the English-language treaties they were signing.

WORDS TO KNOW

debt: an amount of money or something else that is owed.

The last great battle started by Native Americans to preserve their way of life took place in 1876. The Sioux and Cheyenne signed the Fort Laramie Treaty with the United States in 1868 because they were promised the Black Hills of the Dakota Territory. The Black Hills were sacred to them, as they had lived and hunted there for many years.

But when U.S. Lieutenant Colonel George Armstrong Custer was traveling through the Black Hills, he saw "gold around the roots of the grass." Gold diggers hoping to get rich poured into the area, setting up camps and destroying Native American land.

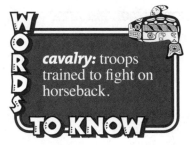

U.S. leaders wanted to buy the land, but the Native Americans refused to sell it. So the government simply broke the Fort Laramie Treaty. In March 1876, U.S. troops moved into the region to take over the lands. Led by two Lakota chiefs, Sitting Bull and Crazy Horse, nearly 3,000 Native Americans gathered to fight the troops. They managed to kill about 225 of Custer's soldiers and drove the U.S. troops back. Word of the Battle of the Little Bighorn, also known as Custer's Last Stand, spread quickly, and **cavalry** from all over the United States poured into the area to help defeat the remaining Native Americans.

WORDS TO KNOW

cavalry: troops trained to fight on horseback.

Crazy Horse and Sitting Bull continued to fight, but eventually were forced to give up and move onto reservations. They were among the last great Native American chiefs to surrender. Crazy Horse was killed the following year.

LEARNING MORE

All Native American tribes in all regions have experienced a great deal of change. From the Northeast Woodlands across the Great Plains to the Pacific Northwest and everywhere in between, once powerful tribes were defeated. Today, the descendants of these tribes continue to work to keep their heritage alive through museums, archaeological digs, cultural centers, and more.

Some still live on one of the 334 reservations in the United States, while others live in neighborhoods and cities just like you. They continue to fight with the United States government for their property rights.

> ❊ **The descendants of many Native Americans have begun to tell the stories of their ancestors to people outside their tribes. This is helping non-Native Americans understand history from a Native American perspective.**

DID YOU KNOW?

The largest mountain carving in progress honors Crazy Horse. It has been under construction in the Black Hills of South Dakota since 1948. When it is finished in 2020, it will be 563 feet tall (171 meters) by 641 feet long (195 meters).

Archaeological digs continue to unearth artifacts that help reconstruct these people's ways of life, and some of their old settlements have been declared National Historic Sites. Pottery, blankets, baskets, jewelry, tools, and other Native American artifacts are in museum collections across the country. Some facilities have even recreated entire villages where you can learn about the day-to-day life of traditional Native Americans.

At the start of the 1900s, Native Americans were known as the "Vanishing Americans." Now, more than a century later, they are one of the fastest growing populations in the United States. As of 2010, there were more than 5 million Native Americans living in the United States and the number is rising.

Native Americans

Finding Names from History

Although many Native American tribes no longer live on their homelands, many place names all across the country remind us of their former presence.

Following are some tribes whose names are still used, in whole or in part, to describe locations. Look at this map and on maps online to see how many places you can find that resemble the following tribal names. What can you find in your own home state?

• Aleut	• Erie	• Mohave	• Spokan
• Cheyenne	• Illinois	• Montauk	• Susquehannock
• Columbia	• Kansa	• Narragansett	• Tuscarora
• Dakota	• Massachuset	• Osage	• Wichita
• Delaware	• Missouri	• Penobscot	

[Map of the United States with states labeled: WASHINGTON, OREGON, IDAHO, MONTANA, NORTH DAKOTA, MINNESOTA, WISCONSIN, MICHIGAN, VERMONT, NEW HAMPSHIRE, MAINE, NEW YORK, MASSACHUSETTS, RHODE ISLAND, CONNECTICUT, PENNSYLVANIA, NEW JERSEY, DELAWARE, MARYLAND, WEST VIRGINIA, VIRGINIA, OHIO, INDIANA, ILLINOIS, IOWA, SOUTH DAKOTA, WYOMING, NEBRASKA, NEVADA, CALIFORNIA, UTAH, COLORADO, KANSAS, MISSOURI, KENTUCKY, TENNESSEE, NORTH CAROLINA, SOUTH CAROLINA, ARIZONA, NEW MEXICO, OKLAHOMA, ARKANSAS, ALABAMA, GEORGIA, TEXAS, LOUISIANA, MISSISSIPPI, FLORIDA, HAWAII, ALASKA]

Glossary

adapt: to make changes to survive in new or different conditions.

adobe: a building material made of sun-dried earth and sometimes straw.

adze: a tool similar to an ax used for trimming and shaping wood.

agricultural: based on farming.

Americas: the lands of North and South America.

ancestors: people from your family or culture that lived before you.

Antarctica: the land around the South Pole that is one of the seven continents. It is south of 66 degrees latitude south.

aqueduct: a large pipe or conduit bringing water from a distant source.

archaeologist: a scientist who studies ancient people and their cultures through the objects they left behind.

Archaic Period: the name given by archaeologists to the earliest periods of a culture.

Arctic: the region around the North Pole within the Arctic Circle.

Arctic Circle: the Arctic Ocean and the surrounding land north of 66 degrees latitude north.

artifact: an ancient, man-made object.

artisan: a skilled worker who makes things by hand.

awl: a small, pointed tool used to make holes, especially in leather.

BCE: put after a date, BCE stands for Before Common Era and counts down to zero. CE stands for Common Era and counts up from zero. These non-religious terms correspond to BC and AD.

Beringia: an exposed mass of land that scientists believe once connected Asia and the Americas.

bison: the correct name for an animal called the buffalo.

blubber: the fat of whales and other sea mammals.

breed: to produce babies.

British colonies: the early English settlements in America.

carbon-14 testing: a scientific method for determining an artifact's age based on the amount of carbon 14 it still contains.

caribou: a deer from the Arctic and just south of the Arctic, also called a reindeer.

causeway: a raised road across water or wet ground.

cavalry: troops trained to fight on horseback.

chickee: a Seminole home built with plant materials in the swamps of Florida.

chisel: a hand tool with a sharp, wedge-shaped blade used to cut or shape wood and stone.

cistern: a large tank for storing water.

civilization: a community of people that is advanced in art, science, and politics.

climate: the average weather patterns in an area over a long period of time.

coexistence: living together.

colonist: a settler living in a new land.

confederacy: a group of people, states, or nations that comes together for a common purpose.

corn silk: the long, silky fibers that hang out of a corn husk.

crop: a plant grown for food and other uses.

cultivate: to prepare and use land for growing food.

culture: the beliefs and way of life of a group of people.

currency: something that can be used to trade or pay for goods.

customs: traditions or ways of doing things, including dress, food, and holidays.

debris: the remains of anything broken down or destroyed.

debt: an amount of money or something else that is owed.

descendant: related to someone who lived in the past.

devastating: highly destructive or damaging.

driftwood: broken pieces of wood floating in the sea or a river that wash up on a beach or riverbank.

drought: a long period of time without rain.

endurance: the ability to withstand something difficult for a long time.

environment: a natural area with plants and animals.

Eskimo: an insulting nickname given to the northernmost Native Americans by the Algonquian tribes from the south.

evaporate: when a liquid heats up and changes into a gas.

evidence: something that proves, or could prove, the existence of something or the truth of an idea.

excavate: to dig up.

extinct: when a group of plants or animals dies out and there are no more left in the world.

Glossary

famine: a period of great hunger and lack of food for a large population.

fertilize: to join female and male cells to produce seeds and offspring.

food chain: a community of animals and plants where each different plant or animal is eaten by another plant or animal higher up in the chain.

forage: to search for food.

Formative Period: a period defined by the development of agriculture, the establishment of permanent settlements, and the development of the arts.

foundation: the base of a home that is partly underground and supports the weight of the building.

glacier: a huge mass of ice and snow.

gouge: a chisel with a curved, hollowed blade used to cut grooves or holes in wood.

graze: to eat grass.

gully: a deep, narrow valley between hills or mountains.

harpooner: someone who hunts using a harpoon, a weapon with a sharp end that is thrown into an animal's body.

heptagonal: something with seven sides.

herd: a large group of animals.

heritage: a culture passed down through generations.

hide: the skin of an animal.

hieroglyph: a symbol in a written language that uses pictures and symbols to represent words or ideas.

horizon: the line in the distance where the land or sea seems to meet the sky.

hostile: very unfriendly, relating to an enemy.

Ice Age: a period of time when ice covers a large part of the earth.

igloo: a dome-shaped structure built of blocks of packed snow.

immigrant: a person who moves to a new country to settle there permanently.

ingenuity: the ability to solve difficult problems creatively.

inherit: to acquire something from an ancestor.

inlaid: when one material is set into the surface of another material to create a design.

insulate: to keep the heat in and the cold out.

irrigation: moving water through canals, ditches, or tunnels to water crops.

kashim: a ceremony house used by Inuit men.

kayak: a long narrow boat covered in animal skin. The paddle has a blade on each end.

kiva: a large room partially underground used for religious and other purposes.

latitude: imaginary lines around the earth that measure a position on the earth north or south of the equator.

leister: a fish spear with three prongs.

longhouse: the traditional building that housed several Iroquois families.

lure: to attract an animal.

magnetite: a type of iron ore in which you can sometimes see your reflection.

maize: corn.

maneuver: a movement requiring skill and care.

mascot: a symbol of an organization.

meal: the edible part of a grain, ground into a powder such as cornmeal.

megafauna: an animal weighing more than 100 pounds (45 kilograms).

mesa: a wide flat area on top of a hill with one or more cliff-like sides.

Mesoamerica: the region that includes parts of Mexico and Central America.

microscopic: something so small it can only be seen with a microscope.

migrate: to move from one place to another, usually with the change of seasons.

moccasin: a shoe made of soft, flexible leather or animal skin.

natural resource: something found in nature that is useful to humans, such as water to drink, trees to burn, and fish to eat.

negotiate: to reach agreement by discussion.

nomadic: moving from place to place to find food.

octagonal: eight sided.

overpopulation: when there are too many people in an area.

palisade: a fence made of rows of pointed posts.

pigment: a substance found in nature that can be used to give color to paint.

pilgrim: a person who travels for religious reasons.

potlatch: a ceremony, sometimes lasting for several days, at which a host lavishes gifts upon the guests.

preserve: to keep fresh or safe.

Glossary

pueblo: a communal village consisting of one or more flat-roofed structures of stone or adobe, arranged in terraces and housing a number of families.

quahog: a thick-shelled clam.

radioactive element: a chemical substance made of one type of atom that changes because its positively charged particles escape from its center over time.

rebellion: an act of open or violent resistance.

relic: an item used by people in an earlier time.

representative: a single person who speaks for the wishes of a group.

reservation: public land set aside for a special use, such as for the relocation of Native Americans in the 1800s.

retreat: to move away from danger.

Roman Empire: the empire that ruled the area of the world from Britain and Germany to North Africa and the Persian Gulf from about 27 BCE to 393 CE.

rotunda: a round structure.

sacred: highly valued and important.

sacrifice: to kill a person or animal as an offering to a god.

sapling: a young tree.

savage: fierce, uncontrolled, and ferocious.

semiprecious: minerals that can be used as gems but are considered less valuable than precious stones.

settler: a person who is one of the first to live in an area.

silo: an airtight pit or tower in which food can be stored.

sinew: a strong band of animal tissue that connects muscles to bones.

snare: a trap attached to a trigger, designed to entangle animals.

society: an organized community of people.

sod: a section of earth with growing grass and roots.

spawn: to produce and deposit eggs.

species: a group of plants or animals that are closely related and look the same.

staple: an important part of a diet.

stelae: upright stone slabs or pillars carved with inscriptions or designs to record dates and important information about the Maya rulers. Singular is stela.

surplus: extra; more than what is needed.

sustainable: living in a way that has minimal long-term impact on the environment.

sustenance: something, especially food, that supports life or health.

syllabary: a set of characters representing syllables that is used like an alphabet.

tipi: a cone-shaped tent made with poles covered by animal skins or bark.

Thanksgiving: a name given to the feast shared by the Native Americans and Pilgrims after the harvest of 1621.

thatch: straw, leaves, or any similar material used for making a roof.

theory: an unproven idea used to explain something.

toll: a charge to use a passageway, such as a river, road, or bridge.

totem: a carved or painted picture or symbol, often representing a family or clan with a reminder of its history.

totem pole: a pole or post carved and painted with totems.

trade: to exchange goods for other goods or money.

traditional: a belief, custom, or way of doing things that has been passed on from generation to generation for a long time.

travois: a sled consisting of a net or platform dragged along the ground between two poles that are pulled by a horse or dog.

treaty: a formal agreement between two parties relating to peace, trade, and/or property.

tribe: a large group of people with common ancestors and customs.

troops: soldiers.

Wampanoag: Native Americans of Massachusetts, from the Algonquian words *wampa*, meaning "dawn," and *noag*, meaning "people."

wampum: shell beads used in ceremony or to trade.

wattle and daub: a type of house construction made by weaving a frame of rivercane, wood, and vines that is coated with a mud plaster and a thatch or bark roof.

wealth: a large amount of money or great number of possessions.

weir: a fence or obstruction built in a river or stream to divert water or catch fish.

whelk: a large marine snail.

wigwam: the rounded or rectangular home of the Algonquian tribes.

wilderness: land that is not settled or changed by people.

Resources

✦ Web Sites

500nations.com
choctaw.org
ftmcdowell.org

hopi-nsn.gov
mohegan.nsn.us
narragansett-tribe.org

navajopeople.org
seminoletribe.com
wmat.nsn.us

✦ Museums, Monuments, and Sites to Visit

Go to nomadpress.net for a more extensive list.

Russell Cave National Monument, Alabama. Tour with a ranger who demonstrates tools, weapons, and Native American ways of life.
nps.gov/ruca/index.htm

Anchorage Museum of History and Art, Alaska. Changing events are geared toward hands-on learning.
anchoragemuseum.org

Pueblo Grande Museum, Arizona. Located at a 1,500-year-old Hohokam village ruin. Guided tours are available, and a museum and store are on site.
pueblogrande.com

Denver Museum of Nature and Science, Colorado. The North American Indian Cultures exhibit includes a reconstructed snow house, Northwest Coast clan house, Navajo hogan, and Cheyenne teepee.
dmns.org

Ah-Ta-Thi-Ki Seminole Museum, Florida. Regular exhibits and a living Seminole village.
ahtahthiki.com

Nez Perce National Historical Park, Idaho. This park comprises 38 sites in Idaho, Oregon, Washington, and Montana that commemorate the stories of the Nez Perce people. Scavenger hunts and walking tours are among the activities that families can enjoy together.
nps.gov/nepe/

Mitchell Museum of the American Indian, Illinois. Nearly 10,000 objects and more than 5,000 books about Native American history and culture.
mitchellmuseum.org

Effigy Mounds National Monument, Iowa. This site includes several types of mounds, including animal effigy, bird effigy, and conical and linear types.
nps.gov/efmo/index.htm

Peabody Museum of Archaeology and Ethnology, Massachusetts. One of the oldest and largest collections of cultural objects in the Western Hemisphere.
peabody.harvard.edu

Nelson-Atkins Museum of Art, Missouri. A collection of Plains and Southwest Native American artworks including Navajo blankets, Pueblo pottery, and California basketry. Classes and events are scheduled regularly for adults and children.
nelson-atkins.org

Indian Pueblo Cultural Center, New Mexico. Showcases the history and accomplishments of the Pueblo people from pre-Columbian days to the present. More than 200,000 people visit each year.
indianpueblo.org

American Museum of Natural History, New York. Permanent exhibitions include the Hall of Northwest Coast Indians and the Hall of Eastern Woodlands and Plains Indians.
amnh.org

National Museum of the American Indian, New York and Washington, D.C. Exhibitions, events, and student and family programs.
nmai.si.edu

Carnegie Museum of Natural History, Pennsylvania. The Alcoa Foundation Hall of Native Americans focuses on the Tlingit of the Northwest Coast, the Hopi of the Southwest, the Lakota of the Plains, and the Iroquois of the Northeast.
carnegiemnh.org/exhibitions/amindians.html

Crazy Horse Memorial, South Dakota. This memorial includes the Indian Museum of North America, the Native American Cultural Center, a sculptor's studio, and more.
crazyhorse.org

Northwest Museum of Arts and Culture, Washington. The permanent collection includes one of the nation's finest groupings of Plateau Native American artifacts. Works of living Native American artists also are highlighted.
northwestmuseum.org

Index

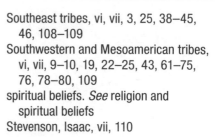